The Brain and Educational Connections

Bridget Connor

University Press of America,® Inc.

Lanham • Boulder • New York • Toronto • Plymouth, UK

To

Diane Bardol, GNSH

Kathleen Marie Engers, SSND

Contents

List of Figures

List of Tables

Chapter One

Predisposed for Intelligent Life

PART I

Learning, and therefore education, is effective when it builds on the natural order. Educational benefits will be realized by understanding and respecting innate human abilities. If there is a curriculum and learning environment that is complementary, natural brain development will be enhanced. One of the first evolutionary concepts is that change is an expected norm and that this change is necessary for development and survival of the species. The process of evolution, as we understand it, moves from the simple to the more complex, from the single cell to the multi-cell organism.

Developing from the simple to the complex is at the heart of the Theory of Emergence (Holland, 1998). Evidence supports this idea of simple to complex development in the universe and here on earth. Early research that provides credence to the theory of emergence is in the lab experiments that produced amino acids as the possible precursor to life forms. In a classic experiment, earth's readily available elements were used to demonstrate that amino acids, the building blocks of life, will, in the right environment, self-organize. The classic 1953 Miller-Urey experiment used methane ($CH4$), ammonia ($NH3$), hydrogen ($H2$), and water ($H2O$), all resources thought to be available more than 3.5 billion years ago here on earth. This experiment produced amino acids and other essential elements needed for life. It was a major discovery in bridging our understanding of the inorganic to the organic. It is thought that these early experiments uncovered the possible precursors to life. Early earth volcanic eruptions provided other gases, adding to the possibility of greater diversity in chemical arrangements and therefore adding to the pool of early beginnings. It is believed that a chemical system evolved through a step-wise (first step needed in order to proceed to the second step) process in such a way that transformed the inorganic to organic. This evolutionary process is what we enjoy today as life (Hazen, 2005).

Some of the same simple readily available elements, carbon (C), hydrogen (H), nitrogen (N), oxygen (O), and phosphorus (P), are needed for the more complex structure of DNA. The backbone structure of DNA consists of a sugar (C, H, and O) and a phosphate (P, O). This backbone supports the base pairs, Adenine (A) and Thymine (T), Cytosine (C) and Guanine (G), of DNA. (See Figure 1.1) The base pairs have different arrangements using no more than four elements (N, H, O and C), part of the simplicity and yet complexity of life (Hazen, 2005). Emergence systems "are composed of copies of a relatively small number of components that obey simple laws. Typically these copies are interconnected to form an array that may change over time" (Holland, 1998, p. 225). The complex double helix is composed of a relatively small number of components that interconnect to form an array. DNA, though quite complex, follows a repeated design.

Hazen (2005) described a marvelous example of a mechanism that developed in the right combination to support life. He stated that one of the "challenges in understanding life's emergence lies in finding mechanisms by which just the right combination of smaller molecules was selected, concentrated and organized into the larger macromolecular structures" (p. 141). One such smaller molecule is

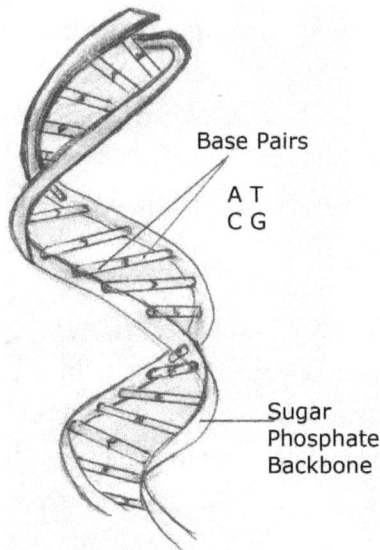

Base Pairs

A T
C G

Sugar
Phosphate
Backbone

Figure 1.1. Double Helix

the lipid. To understand the importance of the lipid to cell develop-ment, it is essential to understand the nature of water. Water is known as one of the most effective solvents. Given time, it will break down most anything in the environment. Since water is also a necessity of life as we know it, a system of maintaining cell integ-rity and allowing for the presence of water is required. Lipid cells are amphiphilic, that is, they both love water and hate water. The molecules combine in just the right manner so as to maintain the cell's integrity. These cells self-organize so that they thrive in a watery environment. Hazen cited Bangham's early 1960 experi-ment with egg-yoke. Bangham observed that the egg-yoke lipid cells that were immersed in water spontaneously organized. The cells' molecules arranged in a way to keep the water on the outside quite separate from the water on the inside. Hydrophilic molecules (lover of water) encircled the outside of the cell. They were joined with the inner molecules, hydrophobic, or water resistant mole-cules. These inner molecules that needed protection from the water

were once again encircled by the very inner most hydrophilic molecules protecting the inner covering of the membrane. In this manner, the cell membrane maintained its integrity allowing for water
substances on the inside and outside. The encircling of the cell with
this type of arrangement was observed to develop spontaneously.
This kind of self-organization, still a precursor to life, is another
example to support the concept of emergence theory, simple beginnings yet step-wise process to complexity (Hazen, 2005). Self-organization appears to be innate.

There is organization within the cell. In a typical high school
experiment, students quickly realize the importance of the nucleus
of a cell. An amoeba can be cut into pieces and still thrive. It is only
when the nucleus is removed that the amoeba dies. This kind of
experiment gives evidence that the nucleus contains the essential
elements to keep the amoeba alive and reproduce. Further experiments isolated DNA as the specific material within the nucleus that
actually coded for life.

Continued research of the nucleus and DNA of species would
finally bring us to the Human Genome Project. This project studied
each chromosome and the DNA structure to determine the full
compliments of base pairs of ATCG. The Human Genome is made
of approximately 3 billion base pairs of ATCG. There are 46
chromosomes. Each cell has a complete set of chromosomes (23
pairs). Number 23 chromosome determines the sex. (See Figure
1.2) Examples of the relationship among chromosomes, genes, and
base pairs are as follows. Chromosome #7 has approximately 1880
genes and more than 150 million base pairs. Chromosome #11 has
more than 2000 genes over 130,000,000 base pairs. Chromosome
#22 has about 800 genes with more than 40,000,000 base pairs.
Each chromosome has its unique number of genes and each gene
has its own combination of base pairs. For details of each chromosome and related diseases see the National Institute of Health
(NIH) at http://www.ncbi.nlm.nih.gov/books/NBK22266/

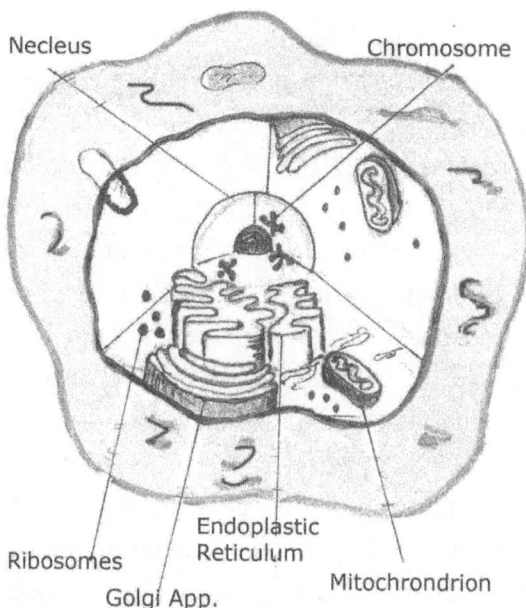

Figure 1.2. Cell Interior

Although the exact number of genes is debated, a general acceptance is that all 23 chromosomes have an approximate number of 24,000 genes. The arrangement, AT and CG, within all of the genes provides us with the approximate three billion base pairs. Our genes (and base pairs) hold the potential for the expression of who we are. Our genes are passed down to us. They are our heredity. They make up who we are. Not all genes are expressed. Those that are expressed are called phenotypes. Typically dominant genes are expressed. Understanding inheritance advanced through experimentation.

Initially it was thought that the new offspring had no trace of the parents, that the new offspring was a blending of the parents. If, for example, a red tulip was pollinated with a white tulip, a pink tulip was expected. It was thought that the newly formed pink tulip had no traces of either the white or red coloring of the tulip parent. In other words, there was no knowledge that the recessive gene existed. Mendel's work countered the idea that an offspring was a blending of the parents and that the offspring left no trace of the original. He was able to determine from his work with peas that offspring inherited distinctive genes from each parent. The possibility of expressing parent characteristic was actually numerical. The offspring has the possibility of receiving two dominant genes (TT), two recessive (tt) or one dominant and one recessive (Tt or tT). Two recessive genes, one from each parent, will generally have the possibility of being expressed 25% of the time, giving the advantage of expression to the dominant genes. This follows a pattern that can be numerically calculated. The phenotype, or the dominant parent characteristic, will be expressed 75% of the time. Such physical features as eye color, freckles, dimples, ear lobes are numerically represented in the population and inherited. Albinism requires two recessive genes, so as generations become removed from the previous, so the numerical expression of albinism becomes less. It is also true that the dominant gene will continue to increase in its expression over generations. Mendel's work established the concept of heredity and the passing on of genes. This was understood early by farmers and animal breeders. Farmers were quick to develop the most productive plants and the trees with the sweetest fruits. In the animal world desirable traits have been carefully selected, such as speed for horses (Pierce, 2005).

Other traits, such as temperament, as seen in the Russian feral fox experiment, surprised scientist. They did not expect that these feral foxes would have an ability to change a temperament trait in such a short time (3 generations). A geneticist was employed to assist in the development of a more friendly fox. Foxes with gentle disposition were selected for breeding. In a relatively short time span, foxes that were bred for this gentle disposition were able to receive human affection and respond to a name. They were much easier to handle. Physical and chemical changes were evidenced. These changes came as somewhat of a surprise. Dopamine, melatonin, adrenaline, color of fur and shape of ears were all measurably different. This study supported that it is possible to control certain factors in animals by the care given to them and selective breeding (Sherman, P. (Ed.), 2010). The environment could indeed influence genetics.

Additional studies examined other factors that were related to genetics. In a study involving seven pairs of fraternal twin goats, it was not just genetics, but again evidence that the environment and genetics were also predictors of timidity. The twin goats were separated at birth. One twin from each of the seven pairs was reared with other goats as usual while the other twin from each of the seven pairs was reared by humans. A scale of timidity was developed. While timidity was different in each set, those reared by humans were all less timid; however, the order or rank of timidity was the same among siblings, so that if the first twin were #1 in timidity scores so too was the other twin #1 reared in the other situation. Genetics clearly was evidenced in these results. Genes matter but changes could be brought about by the environment (Lyons, Price and Moberg, 1988).

In other areas innate skills or abilities are present. There is no training needed to teach imprinting to a chick. Imprinting of baby chicks with the mother is spontaneous and automatic. The baby chick follows the first moving object, generally the mother hen. It is a phenomenon that happens. There are also skills or particular steps that certain dogs seem to know without being taught. Dogs, such as the Australian shepherd, while still better skilled through training, seem to have herding abilities from birth (Hagerty, 2014).

Genetics certainly matter when things go wrong. While mutations can bring about positive changes, as more often happens, there are devastating effects when mutations negatively affect the gene pool. Such devastating effects of mutant base pairs can cause severe damage and often death. For instance, the NIH government site reports on the following three genetic brain diseases that have particular chromosome mutations

- Chromosome #15—Mutations in the *HEXA* gene causes Tay-Sachs disease, destroys nerve cells (neurons) in the brain and spinal cord.
- Chromosome #12—Phenylketonuria (PKU)—The body can't process part of a protein called phenylalanine—this results in severe intellectual disability.
- Chromosome #17—Leukodystrophies are rare diseases that affect the cells of the brain. Specifically, the diseases affect the myelin sheath (ASPA gene).

(Source: National Institute of Health (NIH), http://www .nlm.nih.gov/medlineplus/)

Scientists and doctors do all that they can to address human tragedies. It is known, for instance, that the P53 gene in the lungs is destroyed by certain chemicals found in tobacco. Genetic engineering can replace the cancerous P53 gene with a healthy gene. This has already met with some success in patients with fourth stage lung cancer (NIH). Other advances are being made. Genetic defects are detected early and treated early. Universal infant screening can detect up to 80 differing diseases and developmental problems.

Genetics gone wrong can limit one's capabilities and yet genetics hold great potential and possibilities. Our genetics predisposes us toward innate abilities. In *Origins of Intelligence in Children* Piaget (1971) identifies two particular innate abilities of the child, organization and patterning. We are not born to learn these abilities but rather already have the capacity innately to organize, recognize, and use patterns. Patterning and organizing are things we do. Piaget wrote, "It is by adapting to things that thought organizes itself and it is by organizing itself that it structures things" (p. 8). Piaget's observations of the infant and child seem to parallel the concepts presented in emergence theory.

Other abilities are innate and passed on through ancestry. One clear example of this is species response to threat. Single organisms react to danger, such as too much light or heat. Complex organisms of different species all have a survival circuit. Le Doux (2012) wrote, "specific . . . circuits are innately wired into the brain by evolution and these mediate functions that contribute to survival and well-being of the organism" (p. 654) and again "threat detection involves processing of innate and learned threats by the nervous system via transmission of information about the threat through sensory systems to specialized defense circuits" (p. 656). Le Doux noted several brain areas of activation in threat responses but specifically identified research that indicated that the amygdala nuclei are active and involved in responding to threats. This was so for reptiles, rodents, and primates, including humans. He specified that response patterns are genetically hard-wired. Survival demands that species notice what is different in their environment. Noticing a predator could mean life or death. Novelty is noticed for survival sake and is an innate ability. Predicting what will come of the new environment is equally important to survival. Education can clearly gain by using the natural ability to notice things out of the ordinary and to figure out what is next. Organization, pattern making, observing differences, and making predictions are innate abilities.

Certain abilities, such as the use of our eyes, are considered "experience expected" abilities. In other words, if you have the opportunity to use your eyes then eyesight is to be expected and good eyesight will develop. But if the experience is not provided, as for instance, fish that live within the darkness of deep sea caves all of their lives, even though they have eyes, they cannot see. An educational environment that provides experiences to support natural development will have positive consequences.

Genetics matters and can go awry, certainly environment can limit even more so. An abusive and neglectful environment can be compared to a death sentence. The Romanian orphanages shortly after World War II are examples to the world of just what environment can do to limit the gene potential and a child's development.

See ABC 20/20 episode at http://www.youtube.com/watch?v=
RuO0B56evT0. Proper environments are essential to the natural
order of development.

Genetics matters, but then against all odds there are stories that
evidence a different outcome. In the rare occasion when genetics
appears to be the limiting factor, a story arises that seemingly
contradicts this idea of limitation. The documentary on the life of
Leslie Lemke was originally aired on television as a part of the
show, "That's Incredible in 1981." The married couple, Mary and
Joseph, adopted Leslie as an infant. It was believed that Leslie
would die at a very early age and surely never walk or talk. The
PBS presentation aired the infant's story, now a grown man. See
the story at http://www.youtube.com/watch?v=RuO0B56evT0. Not
only did he outlive his predicted lifespan, but he was a savant who
heard a musical score and instantly played that score. The pleasure
he brought to so many through his ability to play the piano paled in
regard to the joy he brought to his parents.

In another culture, an African tribe receives a child who is "different" as a gift. There is great wisdom and compassion in a people
that showers graciousness and care on those who are seen as less
fortunate than themselves.

Universal screening and genetic engineering have a very positive role in humanity but can also have the power to destroy. The
information from the screening of the unborn, for instance, can and
is used to terminate life. The systematic decisions to eliminate the
Jews during World War II, because they did not fit what some
thought worthy of life, is another mark of human horror. Decisions
like these can systematically hinder the emergence of life and can
debilitate a society. A systematically supported callous decision to
kill the fetus or a group of people because they were not deemed fit
to live, destroys the very essence of what it means to be human,
because it systematically erases the developmental process of a

compassionate people. Genetics is our gift; epigenetics (gene and environment development) is our responsibility.

PART II

The evolutionary process and evidence of human development support the emergence theory. The human has systems within systems. The health of each system is needed for the other. The Cardiovascular System supplies blood to the body. No blood, no life. Transportation, protection, and maintaining balance or homeostasis are among the critical functions of the circulatory system. Blood carries the necessary oxygen and nutrients. The blood system also removes carbon dioxide and wastes materials from the cells. It transports hormones and other chemicals from chemical origin to target organs. The circulatory system protects us by fighting infection in transporting antibodies. It heals wounds by stopping blood flow. The circulatory system maintains a pH between 7.1 and 7.4. Outside this range we would die. It assists other systems in maintaining body temperature (e.g. closing vessels in extremities when cold). It maintains a balance of electrolytes. It consists of the systemic (artery) circulation and the pulmonary (vein) circulation. If all the vessels could be stretched around the equator, they would circle the earth approximately three times (50,000 miles). Very small vessels, the capillaries, would make up most of the distance. At rest the heart beats about 75 times per minute and with every beat expels about 70 ml of blood (5,250 ml/minute). Moderate exercise will increase a healthy heart-beat to 150 times per minute and pump 140 ml per beat or 21,000 ml per minute. That would be similar to pouring 200 liters of soda down the sink in a minute. Athletes can increase their flow of blood to much higher levels but danger strikes if someone is suffering from arrhythmia; his/her heart will beat up to 300 times per minute.

Chapter 1

The human body at any time will hold five to six liters of blood. Blood consists of erythrocytes (red) cells (45% volume); plasma (55%), which contains blood clotting protein, antibodies, electrolytes (Na, K and chloride) and water (95% of plasma); and leukocytes (1% by volume). There are six types of leukocytes each with its own protective responsibility: Basophils and Eosinophil are associated with allergy responses; Lymphocytes work in concert with the immune system; Megakaryoblasts morph into megakaryocytes, which break up platelets; Monocytes are responsible for eating dead cells and waste material; and Neutrophils fight bacteria. All must be functioning properly or consequences will result. For instance, Hemophilia, a genetic disease, is a condition in which a person does not have the necessary clotting factor. They are missing the blood clotting protein found in blood plasma. At the other end of the spectrum, a deficiency in the protein C causes unwanted clots that can travel to the brain (embolism) and cause a stroke (Marieb & Hoehn, 2009).

The carotid and the basilar arteries supply blood to the brain. The brain's various mechanisms will maintain a constant flow of blood (e.g. baroreceptors in the carotid artery measures blood pressure). The brain does not have an abundant storage system, so blood and glucose in the blood are a constant demand. If there is a drop in blood pressure the brain will cut off supplies to all organs except the heart in order to maintain a steady supply. Previously, death was confirmed when the heart stopped, but now death to cells in the brain because of a lack of oxygen defines death. An artificial heart can pump blood and the person would still be considered alive. Just how long does the brain need to be deprived of oxygen to be considered dead? This has been a source of controversy and often pain for the family members. It has been known that a child who has drowned in very cold water and pronounced dead may actually revive without brain damage. In other cases, because an artificial heart supplies blood to the body for a prolonged period of time, while the patient lies comatose, family members have great difficulty recognizing the death of a loved one. Today the brain is considered central to life and to death.

The brain, about a three-pound organ, is mostly developed at birth. The hard skull bones protect the vulnerable brain. The brain when first studied was sectioned into the midbrain, forebrain, and hindbrain. With increasingly sophisticated instruments the brain structures were further divided. The right and left hemispheres have duplicates of all structures, except for the pineal gland. Because of its uniqueness (one of a kind) early philosophers thought that the soul resided in the pineal gland. While intensive investigation is ongoing, there is much more clarity as to the various functions ascribed to certain brain areas. Using PET, MRI, MEG, and fMRI scans, neuroscientists have determined which brain sites are responsible for certain functions. There is good information at the macro and micro level and more information is constantly clarifying how the brain works.

For the brain to receive and send messages, humans possess a very intricate nervous system. This system is required for survival but, as well, for all that we learn. In order to comprehend the complex Nervous System, a single system, it too is divided into component parts. The two main components are the Central Nervous System and the Peripheral Nervous System. The Central Nervous System includes the brain and the spinal cord. The Peripheral Nervous System is separated into several component parts. It includes all of the nerves that branch out or return to the brain and the spinal cord. The afferent or sensory division includes nerves that are sending messages from the body, such as skin, muscle and joints to the Central Nervous System and nerves that travel from the internal organs (visceral) to the Central Nervous System. The efferent or motor division of the Peripheral Nervous System includes all the nerves that branch from the brain and spinal cord and send messages out to the body. The bottom part of the scull has several openings that allow for nerves to enter and exit the brain. There are twelve major cranial nerves (see Table 1.1).

As indicated by the names of the cranial nerves, there are neural networks that are specific and dedicated to the various senses. Perception depends on the Optic Nerve (II) and these neural networks connect to the Occipital lobe of the brain. The Acoustic Nerves (VII) bring information in from our ears and will make neuronal connections to the temporal lobes. The major Vagus Nerves (X) will help process sensations and make connections to various parts of the brain including the anterior Parietal Lobes. The structure of the nervous system indicates that there are major processes that are important to life and dedication of large areas of the nervous system to uphold those processes.

Table 1.1. Cranial Nerves

I.	Olfactory	sense of smell
II.	Optic	vision
III.	Oculomotor	eye, movement, regulation of pupil size
IV.	Trochlear	eye movement
V.	Trigminal	sensation of the head and face, chewing movements, and muscle sense
VI.	Abducens	abduction of eye, proprioception
VII.	Facial	facial expressions, secretion of saliva, taste
VIII.	Acoustic	1. Vestibular branch—balance or equilibrium sense and 2. Cochlear or auditory branch—hearing
IX.	Glossopharyngeal	taste and other sensations of tongue, swallowing movements, secretion of saliva, aid in reflex control of blood pressure and respiration
X.	Vagus	sensations and movements of organs supplied, for example, slows heart, increases peristalsis, and contracts muscles for voice production
XI.	Spinal accessory	shoulder movements, turning movements of head, movements of viscera, voice production
XII.	Hypoglossal	tongue movements

In Summary

1. Physically and mentally there is an innate ability to organize.
2. Naturally, there is a step-wise process that proceeds from the simple to the complex.
3. Innately, patterns are developed and recognized by the mind.
4. Innately, the mind scans for what is outside expected pattern.
5. Innately, the mind predicts what will happen next in relationship to pattern development and alternatives to the pattern.
6. Genetics is influenced by environment (epigenetics).
7. A proper environment is needed for all learning but also to encourage what is experience expectant.
8. The brain has a constant demand for blood and glucose.
9. Ascending (afferent) and descending (efferent) neural networks are structurally supplied to support sensations and movements.

Educational Connections

Summary points 1–5: We innately, organize, move from simple to complex, search for patterns, observe for the unexpected and predict what will come next.

Gopnik, et al., (2010), and Lucas, et al., (2014) studies support that a natural learning environment for children includes "multiple hypotheses, weighing new possibilities against prior beliefs, experimenting and explaining" (Lucas, 2014, p. 342). Willis (2006) wrote, "Our brains are structured to remember novel events that are unexpected" and "because our brains are encoded to make and respond to predictions, they are particularly stimulated when they predict one effect and experience a different one" (p. 11).

Questions to consider in educational planning:

Does information proceed from simple to complex?
Are there patterns to be discovered?

Are there disruptions to patterns because of additional input?

Is this surprising information interesting enough to be attended to?

Are children encouraged to predict what will happen?

How can you review your materials and present it in a way that encourages student prediction?

Summary points 6–7: Genetics is influenced by environment. Proper learning environment encourages natural development. Willis (2006) wrote, "Learning causes growth of brain cells . . . dendrites increase in size and number in response to learned skills, experiences and information" (p. 1).

Questions to consider in planning the learning environment:

What in the environment impedes learning?

What can you provide in the environment that will increase student curiosity?

What interesting activities are provided to increase student learning skills?

Summary point 8: Blood and glucose to the brain support learning.

How does the educational environment encourage healthy heart and brain?

Summary point 9 addresses the fact that naturally we are provided with billions of neurons for the purpose of controlling action and sensing.

Questions to consider for promoting health and well being:

What in your planning encourages movement?

What in your planning give neuronal exercise to the various senses?

Chapter Two

Exploring Intelligence

We marvel at the accomplishments of men and women throughout history, characters like Da Vinci, Galileo, Curie, Shakespeare, and others. We wonder if they are different and if so how are they different. We search for the reason/s why they were able to accomplish so much. We have been in search of what constitutes intelligence. There are excellent chess players who have amazing memories. Beilock suggested that chess players have no better memories than others but that "Finding meaningful ways to group separate pieces of information into smaller bundles can take the burden off working-memory and help you remember more" (Beilock 2010, p. 54). Basically, chess players use tricks to remember. But then it is not just their memory that makes them successful at chess. Is intelligence creativity, problem solving, good judgment, and/or determination? We need to know what intelligence is if we are to assess it. We have established different assessments to measure intelligence, so there are some elements of intelligence that have been identified. Most of us have been exposed to the standard IQ test. It includes questions of reasoning, reading comprehension, math calculations and other skills that are age appropriate. The results today are based on the average IQ of 100. Fifteen points above or below is one standard deviation from the mean. Ninety-five percent of the population will score between two standards above or below. The origin of the IQ test comes from the work of Alfred Binet (1857–1911), a psychologist, who in 1904 was appointed to the "Commission for the Retarded" in France. A French law had just been enacted for compulsory education for all children, except the blind and deaf. In 1905, Binet with his colleague, Simon, developed what is considered to be the first test of intelligence. One of the reasons for its development was the influence of Bourneville and Charcot, prominent psychiatrists of the day, who were active in providing special classes for children with special needs. Following their lead, Binet wanted a scale that would separate students who needed alternative schooling. The Binet-Simon scale rated students as having normal intelligence for their age or below normal intelligence. As a member of the "Commission for the Retarded," his scale was accepted and used in schools in order to advance the progress made by Bourneville and Charcot for special classes for special needs students. Apparently, Binet had an ulterior motive, legitimizing the role of psychologists in schools, formerly the territory for the psychiatrist. Binet realized the limitations of his scale and said that qualitative input was also necessary (Nicolas, Andrieu, Croizet, Sanitioso, and Burman, 2013). His scale, however, took on a life of its own. Once this scale was transported to the United States and revised by Therman in 1916, it was used for very different purposes.

A second recognized measure of intelligence is the g factor. Charles Spearman (1863–1945), noted for his statistical abilities, combined these abilities with his background in psychology. He was particularly interested in differences in mental abilities. He found that people who performed well on one mental test also performed well on other mental tests. He hypothesized that people were able to draw upon general abilities to do well across tests. Spearmen suggested that this general knowledge, or g factor, has biological basis. In other words, some are born smart and some that are not (Bartholomew, Allerhand, and Deary, 2013, p 223). Beilock (2010) would disagree with such a static view of intelligence. She wrote, "Despite innate differences, our eventual level of success is markedly affected by training and practice" (p 49).

Sternberg (1949–) was one of the first to challenge the well accepted IQ test. He proposed that there is more than one type of intelligence. He recognized three components to intelligence. First he described what he called an analytical intelligence that we use for analyzing, judging, and comparing. Second, there is a creative intelligence. He felt that the standard IQ test never measured creativity. This creative intelligence involved imagining, discovering, and inventing. The third type of intelligence, he referred to as practical intelligence. This kind of intelligence puts ideas into action. Because there are three components in his model, it is called the Triarchic Intelligence Model (Viadero, 1998).

Gardner (2011) also deviated from the well accepted one kind of inherited intelligence and proposed multiple intelligences. He believed that skills vary and that there are multiple ways to solve problems, identifying up to eleven types of intelligences. Some of these include: interpersonal, spiritual, verbal linguistic, mathematical/logical, musical, and spatial. Scales to assess Gardner's multiple intelligences have not been clearly developed, but there are strong proponents of this concept and several schools that are structured to model the theory. Goleman's (1995) theory stands out as unique as he proposes that certain people have a greater degree of emotional intelligence and that emotional intelligence is a better predictor of success than simply the standard IQ. Emotional intelligence enables people to interact and to maintain relationships in their personal and professional lives. This is a very active area of research. A search for emotions and associated brain structures, for instance, will yield hundreds of neuroscience research articles (Le Doux, 2012).

Jensen (2006) described two additional models of intelligences. One he described as similar to the practical intelligence found in Stenberg's model but Jensen called it Street Smarts. There is no measurement that is developed for this type of smarts but Jensen referenced research in describing it. The first study, Carraher, Carraher and Schliemann (1985) posed as customers to five Brazilian youths. Normal sales included calculations of real life problems. After successful street transaction, researchers, asked the youths to take a formal math test. The questions were easier than the street transactions but they were unable to complete the math. A second support of Jensen's idea of street smarts comes from Lehman (1988). In a study involving the use of reasoning and transfer knowledge, Lehman wrote, "The results were shocking: Of the several hundred students tested, many of whom had taken more than six years of laboratory science in high school and college and advanced mathematics through calculus, almost none demonstrated even a semblance of acceptable methodological reasoning about everyday-life events described in ordinary newspaper and magazine articles" (p. 1160). Wagner and Sternberg (1985) also supported this idea of real world knowledge and academic divide. People with street smarts thrive in life but may not do well on any type of IQ test; those who do well in school settings may be at a loss in practical use of knowledge.

The second type of intelligence that Jensen (2006) described is called the Life Quotient (LQ) Concept. He wrote that this kind of intelligence is "having the cognitive ability, domain-specific talents, and real-world motivation to succeed in the world you live in" (p. 34). He noted someone living in New York would need different aptitudes from someone living in an active war-zone. He further wrote, "Volition, mental force, or motivation is another powerful indicator of LQ. You can go a long way in life if you simply won't quit. In fact, many people become world-class experts on something just by working harder at it than anyone else has been willing to work. Again, LQ is three things. First it is the aggregate of the other measures. Second it is the ability to juggle life so that you constantly optimize your outcomes. And finally, it is highly motivated, hard work" (p. 34–35). Determination, then, is central to this type of intelligence.

The ability to measure intelligence presupposes that learning and memories of learning can be retrieved and used for additional purposes. Human abilities for learning and memory are essential, then, to understanding intelligence. Early in life there is a memory that is formed and associated with the self, that is, the name of the child. The child turns when s/he is called. The first recognition of one's own name is evidence of early memories. Remember when your infant cried for an object that you just put away. A few months earlier this may not have happened, but now, the infant has an image or symbol of the toy in his/her mind. There is a memory of the toy. When a child is able to remember that something is missing, s/he has a mental image. Piaget (1971) called this newly acquired skill "object permanence." This memory is associative. The real world is linked with an image. A process is required for an image or a memory to be formed.

Gazzaniga, Ivry, and Mangun (2009) described this process of memory by outlining three stages needed for the successful learning and memory: Encoding, acquisition or the registering of inputs and consolidation requiring representation input; Storage, which is permanent record of information resulting from acquisition and consolidation; Retrieval, which allows for utilizing of stored information (p. 313).

The two main types of memory are referred to as *short-term and long-term memory*. Working memory is considered a type of short-term memory, but Woolfolk (2013) distinguished it from of short-term memory. She wrote, "Short-term memory is not exactly the same as working memory" (p. 289). Short-term memory is the immediate attention that allows one to focus on the present situation and information being presented (15–20 seconds), while working memory is the "interface" of new information and information retrieved from long-term memory (p. 288). Beilock (2010) called working memory the cognitive horsepower (p. 25). She called it the major building block of IQ and a predictor of academic success. Woolfolk (2013) cited a researcher that used the term consciousness as synonymous with working memory. Since working memory, by definition, does not imply long-term memory, it is considered under short-term memory (Gazzaniga, Ivry, and Mangun 2009). Echoic and iconic memories are also considered under short-term memory. They are traces of repeating sounds and sights, respectively, which last only for seconds.

Long-term memory is inclusive of two categories. The first category, declarative memory, is composed of two sub-types, semantic and episodic. Tulving (2002) expanded on the differences between semantic and episodic memory. He wrote:

> Today we think of episodic memory as one of the major neuro-cognitive memory systems (Schacter & Tulving 1994) that are defined in terms of their special functions (what the system does or produces) and properties (how they do it). It shares many features with semantic memory, out of which it grew (Tulving 1984), but it also possesses features that semantic memory does not (Tulving & Markowitsch 1998). (in Tulving, 2002, p. 5)

In referencing episodic memory, Tulving said, "It is the only memory system that allows people to consciously re-experience past experiences" (p. 6). Tulving credits Nielsen's 1958 work for the understanding of the two types of amnesia and therefore two types of remembering. "Nielsen said, 'Amnesia is of two types: (1) loss of memory for personal experiences (temporal amnesia), and (2) loss of memory for acquired facts (categorical amnesia). Either may be lost without the other.' (Nielsen 1958, p. 15)" (in Tulving 2002, p 12). In summary, declarative memory is either semantic memory, which is factual information and not contextual, or it is episodic memory of events in one's personal life and by nature, contextual.

The second type of long-term memory is non-declarative memory, sometimes referred to as implicit memory. Procedural memory is a form of non-declarative memory. This kind of memory does not require one to be conscious of the action. An expert tennis player does not think about his/her form when hitting the ball. The same is true about walking up and down the stairs; one just does it. The ability to walk up and down stairs, although once learned, is now automatic; it becomes an implicit memory. The memory of learning to walk is no longer in the conscious mind. It is a memory we have because we still can do it but it is unconscious or implicit. The same would be true of reading (cognitive skills), or biking, driving, or skiing (motor skills). Other forms of non-declarative memory include:

1. Non-associative learning is learning that we acquire because of repeated performance, such as knowing how to act at a restaurant. After many trips to a favorite restaurant, one knows the proper behavior or what is expected. Repeated exposures to events cause our behavior to become second nature (sensitizing); it is not something that is taught but we are implicitly sensitized to this information through repetition.

2. Classical conditioning involves simultaneously using a stimulus (bell) with an unconditioned response (saliva), such as ringing a bell at the time of meals (Pavlov's dog).

3. Priming prepares a person for future association by being exposed either consciously or unconsciously to stimuli that will later be used to impact recognition (subliminal pictures of popcorn) (Gazzaniga, Ivry, and Mangun 2009).

Whether short-term or long-term, memory is housed in the brain and the brain receives sensory external or internal information at all times. The brain has approximately 100 billion neurons. "Every second a neuron can register and transmit between 250 and 2,500 impulses" (Jensen 2008, p. 11). Each neuron can communicate with more than 5,000 neurons if required.

To help us understand the brain's structure and function, the brain has been labeled into sectional lobes and subunits. While the complete understanding of lobe function is on-going, certain functions are clearly associated with structure. The cerebrum includes the frontal, parietal, temporal, and occipital lobes. The temporal lobe (near our ears) processes sound and smell. It is responsible for part of the process of learning and memory. The reception of sight is housed in the occipital lobe. The occipital lobe (posterior and above the cerebellum) not only processes vision, but also processes the recognition of what we see and its associations with smells, colors, shapes. The parietal lobe recognizes opposite side body part sensations, and contributes to our ability to orient our position in space (right parietal), to determine left from right, to calculate and to write (usually left parietal). The frontal lobe is responsible for attention, planning, judging, and goal setting. The primary motor cortex, which controls movement, is also located in the frontal lobe. Expressive language (Broca's area) is generally housed in the left frontal region of the brain. (See Figure 2.1) The frontal lobe is considered essential for working memory. The cerebellum, located in the back of the brain and just under the occipital lobe, is responsible for balance and coordination of movements. Some lobes are tucked deep within the brain. For instance, the deep nuclei referred to as the basal ganglia, include the caudate, putamen, and the globus pallidus, and contributes to our abilities for movement and sensation. The insular lobe plays a role in movement and sensations. The corpus collosum is the communication network from the right to the left hemispheres and vise versa (Khurana, 2006). The limbic system is inclusive of the thalamus, the hypothalamus (controlling for homeostasis), the hippocampus (essential for consolidation of memories), and the amygdala, which is associated with emotions. The thalamus, itself, acts as a central station for all information received except for olfactory sensations. For example, sight and location information are brought into the optic nerve and then forwarded to the thalamus, which then sends the information to the occipital lobe and onward to other locations. With 100 billion neurons in the brain and upwards of 2,000 impulses transmitted every second from all of our senses, information is processed simultaneously (Jensen, 2008).

In the past century, or more, research and medical procedures have revealed many of the marvels of the brain and deficit implications. Pierre Paul Broca (1824–1880), a French physician, treated stroke patients. One in particular had suffered damage to the left frontal lobe. This patient was able to understand language but had difficulty with speech. Broca was able to identify the exact location of the lesion. This area was then referred to as Broca's area of the brain and associated with articulation (Gere, 2013). Around the same time, Carl Wernicke (1848–1905), a German physician, also

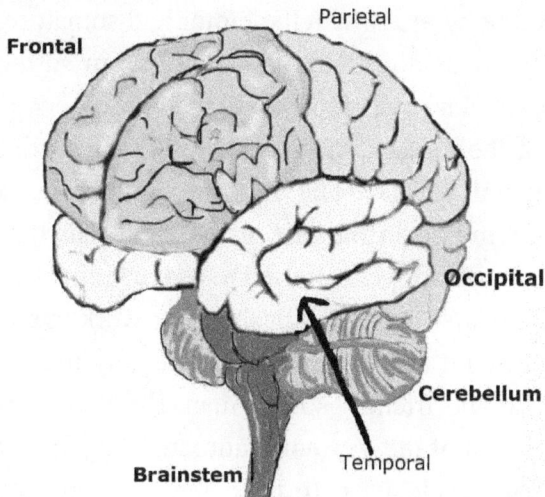

Figure 2.1. Brain Lobes

treated patients with brain injuries. From his work, he was able to distinguish an area of the brain that affected the understanding of language. Lesions to the back part of the superior temporal gyrus clearly were involved with language. This area became known as Wernicke's area (Tomson, A., et al., 2008). In cases of damage to the superior temporal gyrus, the patient spoke but generally made no sense. It was later to be found that these sections of the brain, (Broca and Wernicke's) worked in concert. These early discoveries lead the way for finding specific functions of other brain areas.

Wilder Penfield (1891–1976), one of the early pioneers in the field of neuroscience, treated patients with severe epilepsy through surgery. Patients, under local anesthesia, remained awake during surgery. Penfield stimulated the surface of the brain in the motor and the somatosensory cortex. In this way, he identified the area of the brain that was the cause of the epileptic events and was also able to determine the nerves responsible for affecting other areas of the body. The information that he gathered during these surgeries enabled him to illustrate the surface area of the brain and the nerves that were required for the stimulation of a particular area of the body (Mazzola, L., et al. 2012). He carefully diagrammed the associated affected body areas with the motor and somatosensory cortices. The diagram demonstrated that more brain surface areas are needed for particular parts of the body than for others. For instance, a large part of the motor and the somatosensory cortices are dedicated to the mouth and face and there are more brain neurons dedicated to the thumbs than the rest of the hand. His diagram of the body/brain associations was referred to as the homunculus.

Tragic events also gave insight into the workings of the brain. Phineas Gage by all accounts was an extremely responsible, trustworthy, faithful and friendly sort of man. He worked as a foreman in the construction of the Vermont railroad. The job involved blasting granite with explosives. In checking the explosives, Phineas used a 13-pound rod called a tamping iron. The iron was sharp on one end and flat on the other. On Sept 13, 1848, things went very wrong. The charge went off while Phineas was in the line of danger. The iron rod went through his left check-bone and up into his brain. The doctor could see the hole through his check-bone and left frontal lobe. Phineas remained conscious through this episode, talking to his fellow workers and a half-hour later to the doctor. Strangely enough, he healed from the accident but his personality changed. Physically he was tormented with severe seizures, but more debilitating, he was no longer the responsible caring type fellow but rather a rude, irresponsible, tumultuous stranger. This tragic accident enabled doctors, later, to locate the area of the brain that is associated with making responsible decisions, an area of judgment, setting goals, recognizing right from wrong and planning to execute the proper behavior. These abilities were stolen from Phineas through the accident. No one really recognized him as the person they once knew (Fleischman, 2002). The frontal lobe would hence be associated with planning, organizing and judging.

Clive Wearing, a brilliant musician and director, and happily married man lost access to all his memories as his frontal cortex and hippocampus were destroyed through a herpes virus. See video at http://www.youtube.com/watch?v=ZHUvCR-2AOc. This video demonstrates how the present moment is the only moment that Clive experiences; all relational memory is gone. This case study demonstrates the importance of the hippocampus to the memory system. Sprenger (1999) would refer to the hippocampus as the memory's filing cabinet. The various lobes are responsible for bringing forth past memories, but since Clive's communication system between the frontal lobe and hippocampus was severed, he could retrieve no personal or episodic memories. The frontal lobe is the home of working memory and since this was disengaged from the hippocampus, Clive could also no longer send any new information to the hippocampus for storage. He lived only in the present moment. He knew some facts and could respond; semantic memories could be retrieved. He was able to use his working memory but it was limited since he could not make any connections to his personal or episodic life. His non-declarative memory was also functional. He could, for instance, still play the piano since this demanded the use of his procedural memory. Patients tragically suffer from brain damage, but in that tragedy, neuroscientists, studying the damaged area, can find new understandings of brain structure and function and use that knowledge to help others.

Henry Gustav Molaison, (H. M.) suffered from severe seizures. He elected for a temporal lobectomy. This removed his amygdala and some of his hippocampus. H. M., too, was no longer able to either retrieve his past memories or form new memories that required episodic memory. He was able to form some new semantic and procedural memories. Since semantic memory is initiated by the frontal cortex, his frontal lobe was able to initiate the process of connecting information to other lobes to retain new information. Because the development of procedural memory depends on the health of the motor cortex, basal ganglia and parietal lobes, and they were intact, he could learn some new procedural skills. Working memory functioned as well, since his frontal lobe was intact. All of his past episodic memories, which are dependent on the hippocampus, were gone (Beilock, 2010).

Experimental research of other cases of brain damage has described further discrete areas of the brain and associated functions. Gazzaniga, Ivry, and Mangun (2009) arduously reviewed the literature, reported on H.M., and many other cases, as seen in Table 2.1.

In addition to the study of patients, other efforts were established to study the brain structure, function, and relationship to intelligence. Using methods, such as, PET, MRI, fMRI, MEG scans, neuroscientists have looked at certain locations in the brain that are activated when participants are presented with tasks or problem solving questions. Particular areas of the brain have been identified as activated and therefore needed in order to complete certain tasks.

Table 2.1. Summary of Research (Gazzaniga, Ivry, and Mangun, 2009)

Researcher	Case	Place	Findings
Scotville, W. B., and Milner, B. (1957)	H. M.	Temporal Lobectomy (medial temporal lobe) to stop seizures	-Lost the ability to form new long-term memories particularly episodic -Some new long-term memory intact—possibly semantic memory, e.g. he was able to draw floor plans (p. 333) -Normal short-term memory (sensory and working memory) -5 cm lesion (hippocampus initially thought to be removed but later found to be intact but atrophied) -Could learn procedural task "…showed the inverse pattern" to K.F (p. 325)
Shallice, T., and Warrington, E. (1969)	K. F.	Damage to left perisylvian cortex	-Damage to short-term memory -Could still form types of new long-term memory -"…data support the idea that short-term memory might not be required in order to form long-term memory" (p. 316) -This information differed from the accepted model to that date
Markowitsch, H. (1999)	E. E.	Removed tumor in left angular gyrus—inferior parietal cortex and posterior temporal cortex (similar areas as K.F.)	-Below normal short-term memory for abstract verbal material -Preserved long-term memory -Surprisingly normal visuospatial short-term memory, "The pattern of behavior displayed by these patients (K.F. and E.E.) demonstrates a deficit of short-term memory abilities but a preservation of long-term memory…raised the possibility that short-term memory is not the gateway

			to long-term memory..." (p. 316)
Zola, S., Squire, L. & Amaral, D. (1978)	R. B.	Heart bypass surgery Ischemic episode (reduction of blood to brain p. 327)	-Could not form new-long term memories and lost up to 2 years of past memories -Lesions restricted to particular section (CA1 pyramid cells) of the hippocampus (p. 328) -Supported the idea that the hippocampus is needed for forming new long-term memories
Moscovitch, M., University of Toronto	Alzheimer Patients	Loss of Acetylcholine (Ach) cells that connect to the hippocampus and prefrontal cortex	-Progressive loss of ability to form new episodic memories (p. 330)
Gazzaniga, M. S., (1992)	K. C.	Motorcycle accident—head injury to medial temporal lobe, left dorsolateral prefrontal cortex, premotor cortex, parietal and occipital cortices and diffuse cortical atrophy	-Lost episodic information of his entire life but maintained factual information about his life (how many people in his family) -Verbal fluency deficiency (frontal lobe function) -Normal short term memory -Could learn new facts (semantic memory) -Support that semantic and episodic maybe different memory systems -No deficit in Non-Declarative memory (implicit)—perceptual priming (p 339)
Hamann & Squire (1995)	E. P.	Herpes simplex encephalitis— bilateral damage to medial temporal lobe	-Could not acquire new episodic or semantic information -Could make category judgment (food groups) -Episodic and Semantic memories are not completely separated
Vargha-Khadem, F., Gadian, D, Watkins, K., Connelly, A.,	3 patients	Bilateral injury to the hippocampus	-Problems with episodic memory -Able to form semantic memory -Support that the

Van Paesschen, W., Mishkin, M., (1997)			hippocampus is required for episodic memory
Gazzaniga, M. S., (1992)	Patients taking tranquilizers (benzodiaze-pines)	"Acts on muscarinic acetylcholine receptor" (p. 338)	-Deficits in Declarative Memory -No deficit in procedural memory

Jung and Haier (2007) reviewed 37 neuroimaging studies. Eleven of those studies correlate certain brain areas (frontal and parietal) with performance on the Wechsler Intelligence Scales. While completing other tasks of intelligence, such as deductive reasoning, participants' results also indicated increased brain activity in the frontal and parietal areas. Selected researchers that Jung and Haier examined can be seen in Table 2.2.

Table 2.2.   Summary of Selected Research (Jung and Haier, 2007)

Authors	Research Area	Method	Brain Results
Ingvar, D H., and Risberg, J., (1967)	Cognitive Task	Region al Blood Flow	Gray Matter neuronal activity
Haier, R. J., (2003)	Raven's Advanced Progressive Matrices	PET scan	Neuronal Efficiency correlated with better performance (Lower glucose metabolic rate with high performance)
Parks, R. W., Loewenstein, D. A., Dodrill, K. L., Barker, W.W., Yoshii, F., Chang, J. Y., Emran, A. Apicella, A., Sheramata, W. A., and Dura, R., (1988)	High g load verbal fluency test	PET scan	Temporal and Parietal Lobes and brain efficiencies with higher performance
Ghatan, P.H., Hsieh, J. C., Wirsen-Meurling, A., Wredling, R. Eriksson, L., Stone-Elander, S. Levander, S. and Ingvar, M., (1995)	Perceptual Maze Task (visual spatial reasoning)	Butanol PET	Increase activity in anterior cingulate, medial and right frontal, superior and inferior parietal, inferior temporal and superior occipital lobes
Haier, R. J., and Benbow, C. P., (1995)	Mathematical reasoning (SAT-M)	FDG PET	In men correlations between glucose metabolism in the temporal lobes bilaterally (BA

			20, 21, 22) and High SAT-M Women with High SAT-M did not have increased activity
Goel, V., Buchel, C., Frith, C., and Dolan, R. J., (2000)	Verbal and Non-verbal reasoning (inductive reasoning)	PET	Activation and correlations between Left frontal, temporal, occipital and inductive reasoning (F BA 8, 9, 10, 24, 32, 47, T BA 20, O BA 19) Second study Left frontal (BA 45, 46, 47) Left Temporal (BA 21, 22), Occipital (BA 19) Left cingulate (BA 34, 32) gyri
Esposito, G., Kirby, B. S., Van Horn, J. D., Ellmore, T. M., and Berman, K. F., (1999)	Wisconsin Card Sorting Test and Raven's Progressive Matrices Test (non-verbal reasoning)	PET	Activations and correlations between Dorsolateral Prefrontal (BA 9, 46), Inferior Parietal (BA 39, 40), Anterior Cingulate (BA 32), Inferior/lateral temporal (BA 21, 37) and Occipital Cortices (BA 18, 19) and high scores
Gur, R. C., and Reivich, M., (1980)	Analogical reasoning (high g load)	Xenon Blood Flow	Left hemisphere regions (particularly left inferior parietal cortex and Wernicke's area) and high g loading
Wharton, C. M., Grafman, J., Flitman, S.S., Hansen, E. K., Brauner, J., Marks, A. and Honda, M., (2000)	Visual analogical reasoning	PET	Activation in Left Middle Frontal (BA 6, 8), Inferior Frontal (BA 10, 44, 45, 46, 47) gyri, the anterior insula and the inferior parietal cortex (BA 40) correlated with high reasoning
Duncan, J., Seltz, R. J., Kolodny, J., Bor, D., Herzog, H., Ahmed, A., Newell, F. N. and Emslie, H., (2000)	Reasoning performance (verbal spatial)	Butanol PET	Revised summary Frontal and Parietal (F BA 6, 8, 10, 45, 46, 47 and P BA 7, 40) and also Occipital (BA 18, 19) and high performance
Haier, R. J., Jung, R. E., Yeo, R. A., Head, K., and Alldre, M. T., (2004)	Raven's Progressive Matrices Test (High g loaded test)	PET	High scores correlated with increased activity in bilateral parietal (BA 7), temporal (BA 22, 37) and Occipital (BA 18, 19)
Chen, X. C., Zhang, X. C., Li, Z. H., Meng, X. M., He, S. and Hu, X.P., (2003)	Game of chess and game of GO	fMRI	Chess plays and activations within bilateral regions of parietal (BA 7, 39, 40), Occipital (BA 19) and Left Frontal (BA 6, 8 and 9)

			Go decisions and activation seen in Left Frontal (BA 44, 45), Bilateral Frontal (BA 6, 9), Posterior Cingulate (BA 30, 31), Parietal (BA 7, 40), Temporal (BA 37) and Occipital (BA 19)
Goel, V., and Dolan, R. J., (2001)	Concrete and Abstract relational reasoning problems	fMRI	Acitivation seen in Bilateral Frontal (BA 6, 9), Parietal (BA 7 and 40), Left (BA 17, 18) and bilateral Occipital (BA 19) and Bilateral Subortical Caudate/ Nucleus Accumbens and Cerebellar regions
Noveck, I. A., Goel, V. and Smith, K. W., (2004)	If then symbolic logical and inferences	fMRI	Activation Left Frontal (BA 9, 47), Parietal (BA 40) and Cingualte (BA 32)
Knauff, M., Mulack, T., Kassubek, J., Salih, H. R., and Greenlee, M. W., (2002)	Deductive reasoning "Bob is taller than..."	fMRI	Bilateral Frontal (BA 6, 9), Anterior Cingulate (BA 32), Temporal (BA 21, 22), Parietal (BA 4, 40), and Occipital (BA 19) increased activity and deductive reasoning were associated.
Ruff, C. C., Knauff, M., Fangmeier, T., and Spreer, J., (2003)	Problems of Relational Inference	fMRI	Bilateral Frontal (BA 6, 10), Bilateral Posterior Cingulate (BA 31) and bilateral Occipital (BA 18, 19) as well as Parahippocampus
Gray, J. R., Chabris, C. F., and Braver, T. S., (2003)	Working memory and intelligence	fMRI	Increased activity in Frontal (Left, BA 45, 46, Right BA 4), Parietal (Right 31 and Left 39 and Bilateral 40), Bilateral Temporal (BA 22).
Geake, J., and Hansen, P. C., (2005)	Fluid analogies (letter sequences)	fMRI	Bilateral Frontal (BA 8, 10, 12, 45, 47, and also Left BA 44 Right BA 46), Parietal (BA 7 and 40), Occipital (BA 17, 18)

Other efforts in expanding our knowledge of the brain included autopsy. Korbinian Brodmann (1868–1918), a neurologist, followed some of his patients until after their deaths. With permission, he thoroughly examined their brains after death. He mapped the brain at the cellular level and isolated 52 areas (Gazzaniga, Ivry, and Mangun 2009). A partial listing of Brodmann's areas and location in the brain are 1. Intermediate Postcentral, 2. Caudal Postcentral, 3. Rostral Postcentral, 4. Gigantopyramidal, 5. Preparietal, 6. Agranular Frontal, 7. Superior Parietal, 8. Intermediate Frontal, 9. Granular Frontal, 10. Frontopolar, 11. Prefrontal, 17. Striate, 18. Parastriate, 19. Peristriate, 20. Inferior Temporal, 21. Middle Temporal, 22. Superior Temporal, 37.Ocipitotemporal, 38. Temporopolar, 39. Angular, 40. Supramarginal, 41. Anterior Transverse Temporal, 42. Posterior Transverse Temporal, 44. Opercular, 45. Triangular, 46. Middle Frontal, 47. Orbital (Dubin, 2014). For a complete listing of Brodmann's brain mapping go to: http://spot.colorado.edu/~dubin/talks/brodmann/neuronames.html.

Brodmann's brain areas (BA) are used in describing present day neuroimaging (see Figure 2.2). Several of Jung and Haier's (2007) reviews included BA's so it is helpful to be familiar with these areas. In many of the studies, examined by Jung and Haier, there were clear overlappings of Brodmann's areas. Jung and Haier, using their own research and reviews of major studies, hypothesized the Parieto-Frontal Integration Theory (P-FIT) of Intelligence. They assumed that after receiving and recognizing sensory information generally in the temporal and occipital lobes, the brain forwards information to the parietal cortex. A further assumption on

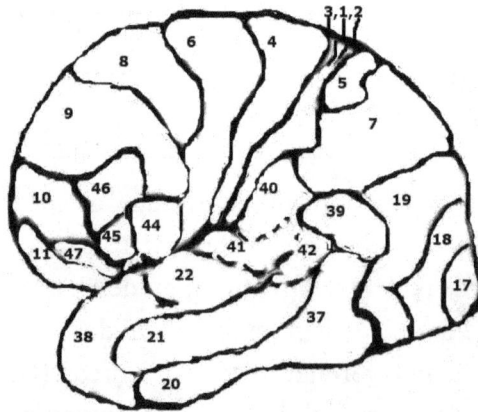

Figure 2.2. Brodmann Areas

their part was that the parietal then interacts with the frontal regions. Jung and Haier identified the P-FIT areas using Brodmann's model. The following steps outline briefly the assumption and processes of Jung and Haier's Parieto-Frontal Integration Theory of Intelligence as outlined on page 138 of their document.

Step 1. Sensory Input

- Information Gathering

  - Primarily through the Visual and Auditory modes
  - Early Processing—Occipital and Temporal Lobes (BA 18, 19)
  - Extrastriate Cortex

- Recognition, subsequent imagery and/or elaboration

  - Fusiform gyrus (BA 37)

- Analysis and/or elaboration of syntax of reading information

  - Wernicke's area (BA 22)

Step 2. Sensory/Perceptual Process then forwards to Parietal Cortex

- Merging of structural symbolism, abstraction, and elaboration

  - Supramarginal (BA 40)
  - Superior Parietal (BA 7)
  - Angular Gyri (BA 39)

Step 3. Parietal Cortex interacts with Frontal Regions

- Hypothesis test to various solutions to a given problem

  - Frontal Regions (BA 6, 9, 10, 45–47)

Step 4

• Engage to constrain response selection and inhibit other competing responses

  • Anterior Cingulate (BA 32)

The P-FIT of Intelligence process is dependent upon "rapid and error-free transmission of data from posterior to frontal brain regions by the underlying white matter" (p. 138).

Jung et al., (2007) also noted that problem solving requiring language clearly activated Wernicke's and Broca's areas, as well as, the angular and supramarginal gyri. They concluded that there are other areas that are likely to be "critical to intelligence" (p. 152). Additional research will either confirm or revise Jung and Haier's theory. Haier, in 2009, wrote, "differing brain profiles may explain why two people with an identical IQ score may show very different cognitive abilities" (p. 4) indicating that activation of brain areas may differ in individuals as they reason or solve the same problems.

Jung and Haier (2007) included examples of patients suffering from lesions (see Table 2.3). This too, gave some support to their theory.

Challenging the P-FIT Theory of intelligence, Blair (2007) commented that the P-FIT model limits its search for intelligence to working memory, executive cognitive abilities including reasoning

Table 2.3. Summary Brain Lesions (Jung and Haier, 2007)

Left Parietal	Lower Verbal Intelligence
Frontal Lobotomy Severing fronto-thalamic white matter Connections—isolating frontal lobe	One point average drop in IQ But adverse effect in judgment, planning and accommodations to novelty
Removal of anterior portions of temporal lobe	Does not appear to affect intellectual performance
Lesion in Wernicke's area	Intellectual decline

abilities but not fluid intelligence. Haier would argue that fluid intelligence is part of the g factor. Blair noted that as tasks become less difficult there is greater use of posterior cortical regions more than frontal ones. "More-expert problem solving requires presumably fewer cognitive resources and exhibits increased parietal activation associated with a more automatic and efficient arrival at problem solution" (p. 155). Haier also wrote of this phenomenon, referred to as brain efficiency. Practice is one strategy that supports brain efficiency.

Further Kadosh, Walsh, and Henik (2007) pointed out "that the activation of this same neuronal network is common to many mental operations that may not be related to intelligence" and that the selected reviews by Jung and Haier "did not control for response selection," such as, including what not to do, which is considered an essential component of intelligence (p. 155).

Jung and Haier (2007) hold that biological mechanisms are responsible for intelligence and that if those areas of the brain can be identified (and corresponding genes) then scientists and educators would have more ability to influence those mechanisms and thereby influence intelligence.

Jensen (2008) outlined a model of how the brain learns new content. While not intelligence per se, learning new content is essential to intelligence.

1. Input begins from our senses or is activated by thinking or memory.
2. Information is first routed to the thalamus for initial processing.
3. Simultaneously, the information is routed to the appropriate cortical structures for further processing (e.g., occipital lobe, temporal lobe).
4. It is also immediately routed to subcortical areas (e.g., the amygdala).

5. If it is an emergency stimulus, the amygdala will respond immediately and recruit other brain areas.
6. Later, information is sent to the hippocampus for more subtle evaluation and held over time.
7. Over time, the hippocampus will organize, distribute and connect the memories with the rest of the appropriate areas of the cortex for long-term storage. High-bias content is more likely to be saved than low-bias information (p. 11).

In Summary

Describing intelligence is somewhat elusive but there are different ways to measure intelligence (Jensen, 2008). Working memory is considered the cognitive workhorse and associated with IQ. While some consider IQ stable, Beilock (2010) explained that working memory can be increased through practice and training and that practice and training increases the neuronal networks throughout the brain. This increases memory overall. Strategies can be taught to increase the ability to remember (Weserberg, & Klingberg, 2007; Lee, Lu & Ko, 2007; Klingberg, 2010). There are three components essential for learning and memory: encoding, storage, and retrieval (Gazzaniga, et al., 2009). The process of encoding, storage, and retrieval takes time. If material is not encoded, it will not go into storage. Pausing and thinking deeply will improve memory (Beilock, 2010). Memory has been categorized into subunits. Short and long-term memories are the two major categories. Studies have found specific areas that are associated with short-term memory. The areas dedicated to short-term memory are different from those specific areas for long-term memory. Episodic and semantic memories seem to have separate but some overlapping neuronal pathways. Episodic, or autobiographical, is memory that is contextual. Processing of information is multi-modal and simultaneous. Brain efficiency is increased with practice. Brain areas are associated with particular brain functions. Lobes are generally associated with particular functions but discrete areas are essential for certain tasks. Examples of discrete areas: 1. Broca's area (BA 44, 45) language—speech—Frontal Lobe; 2. Wernicke's area (BA 22) language—comprehension—Posterior Superior Temporal Gyrus; 3. Motor Cortex (BA 4) descending (efferent) neuronal messages to muscles of the body—Posterior Frontal Lobe; 4. Somatosensory Cortex (BA 1, 2, 3) afferent—incoming messages from bodily sensations (Postcentral gyrus in Parietal Lobe); 5. Pre-Frontal Lobe (BA 9, 10, 11, 12, 46, 47)—executive function, planning, and goal setting.

Gazzaniga, Ivry, and Mangun (2009) concluded:

1. Medial Temporal Lobes, particularly the hippocampus, are essential for rapid consolidation and initial storage of information for episodic and semantic memories (p. 331) and "The medial temporal lobe, then, is not essential for short-term or working memory processes" (p. 343).
2. "Memory is permanently stored in a distributed fashion in the neocortex" (p. 343).
3. The hippocampus is needed for the retrieval of episodic memory but possibly not other types of memory.
4. The left frontal cortex is often found to be involved in encoding of episodic information, whereas the right frontal cortex is often found to be activated in episodic retrieval (p. 353).
5. Encoding and retrieval of semantic memory involves the left frontal cortex (BA 44, 45).
6. "The motor cortex and cerebellum are critical for implicit procedural learning of movement patterns" (p. 356).

Jung and Haier (2007) hypothesized the P-Fit Theory of Intelligence. Jensen offered an additional model of information processing. There is on-going research to develop accurate models that exhibit patterns of functional neuronal networks, but it is clear with supporting research that there are individual differences in brain processing. Further, Beilock (2010) wrote, "Even though the evidence regarding the genetic basis of cognition functioning is compelling, it's important to remember that the environment plays a large role in shaping success" and that heritable traits may be altered with the right brain practice (p. 82).

Educational Connections

Practice and training improves working memory and increases neuronal networks for brain efficiency. Specific strategies can be taught to increase the ability to remember. Encoding information into short-term or working memory and processing it to long-term storage takes time. Learning it well in the first place, establishes longer remembrance. Ebbinghaus's (1913) classic experiment informs instruction. As the sole participant, Ebbinghaus detailed the decay time of non-sense syllable (consonant/vowel/consonant) sounds. The experiment consisted of "163 double tests. Each double test consisted in learning eight series of 13 syllables . . . The learning continued until two errorless recitations of the series in question were possible. The relearning was carried to the same point; it occurred at one of the following seven times—namely, after about one third of an hour, after 1 hour, after 9 hours, 1 day, 2 days, 6 days or 31 days" (p. 312). He found that with each revisit of the words less time was needed for success to recall all syllables. With each successive time for study, increasingly less and less time was needed to recall the list with 100% accuracy. After the seventh study, spread out over weeks, little decay was evident and little time for study was needed. He graphed his research result, which is known as the forgetting curve. Other work, also, supports this idea of less time needed with each successive study period. Price, et al, (2014) wrote that given time and practice, brain processing "became more efficient" (p. 23). Consolidation of material depends on how deeply it was learned in the first place. As noted already, fMRI scans of the brain support the concept of brain efficiency. While Ebbinghaus (1913) demonstrated steps to offset memory decay in non-sense syllables, memory that uses relational context is much more lasting and requires initial focus and attention. Making meaningful connections will transfer information from the working memory to the long-term episodic memory.

Questions for educators:

How do you provide time over weeks, months, to review material that is important to remember in a way meaningful to students?

What kinds of practices have you included to support brain efficiency?

Are these practices of interest to students?

What kind of student connections and relationships to content material are you providing?

What strategies have you introduced to increase skills of memory?

Do students have ideas of how to practice a particular skill?

The cited research supports that the brain is multi-modal and a multi-processor. Willis, (2006) wrote, "offering information visually will set up connections with the occipital lobe . . . having students hear will hook up a dendritic circuit with the temporal lobe . . . the more regions of the brain that store data about a subject, the more interconnection there is" (p. 4). While the brain receives constant information and can process simultaneously, we can only be conscious of one thing at a time. When information is clearly in the working memory, it is only then that this information can be transferred into long-term memory.

How does your instruction provide information that can stimulate the various senses?

Does your instruction often ignore a particular sense?

Is there a way to consider a revision to include this sense?

Are students overloaded with too much stimuli?

How do you consider temperature, sunlight, fresh air in your
teaching environment?

How do you provide the necessary stimuli for students to maintain attention?

How are you arranging your material so that there is only one
focus of attention?

A large part of the brain receives visual information. We are naturally disposed towards visual input. Standing's (1973) research provided participants with 10,000 pictures which they could generally
recall having seen with 90% accuracy. Standing and Bertrand
(2008) reported the "superiority" of picture memory in comparison
to words.

How are pictures and other visual arts included in instruction?

What content connections can be made using imagery?

Episodic memory is contextual. It is all about the "me" memory.

How can you make instruction connect personally?

How can you use the sense of personal connection to assist in
the memory of other material?

Several types of intelligences were described by Gardner (2011),
Goleman (1993), Jensen (2006) and others.

Is there a way to allow students to learn and process information
differently?

Chapter Three

Emotions and Decisions

Some 20 years ago, Noddings (1992) sounded an alarm that our schools were not attending to the greatest needs of our children. Education was dismissing the most important aspect of being human, that of caring. A little later, in the field of neuroscience, Damasio (1998) wrote, "it seems fair to say that emotions must have seemed both too elusive and too subjective to attract the interest of neuroscientists or cognitive scientists concerned with researching that which appeared most concrete and objective" (p. 83). Fourteen years later, Le Doux (2012) wrote, "Emotions is a major research growth area in neuroscience and psychology today" (p. 653). The contributions of Ekman and Goleman have propelled the concept of emotional intelligence. Ekman's (2003), research from around the world established that basic emotions are universal, expressed and recognized by all peoples. There is still, however, disagreement about what the basic emotions are. Feelings and emotions are sometimes used synonymously. The *Webster International Dictionary* defines these words using the same words interchangeably: Feeling—the conditions of one that feels an emotional state, emotional reaction, emotional relationship; Emotions—affective aspect of consciousness, an expression of feeling. Le Doux (1998) stated that "The term feeling should be used to describe the complex mental state that results from the emotional state" (p. 84). Feelings are associated with bodily changes and alterations in cognitive processing. He stated, however, that both can be researched.

Goleman (1995) proposed that the primary families of emotions are anger, sadness, fear, enjoyment, love, surprise, disgust, shame and guilt. Gazzaniga, Ivry and Mangun (2009), citing Ekman, selected a different list for the basic emotions: anger, fear, disgust, happiness, sadness and surprise. While specific basic emotions are still debated, research has established the primacy of emotions, as so clearly seen, when a patient suffers brain damage. A patient, whose prefrontal cortex is disengaged from the amygdala, is no longer able to make simple, everyday decisions or share feelings. While intelligence is still intact, functioning becomes impossible. What should I wear today? What task should I begin with? What appointment should I make first? What if it is our anniversary? No answers to everyday questions simply destroy any relationship and eliminate the possibility of working with others. Successful marriages die and productivity is lost (Goleman, 1995). When feelings or emotions are disconnected from our decisions, so too are preferences. Do you prefer this ice cream or that, this photograph or that? Without feelings we cannot make up our minds. Even simple preferences are based on our feelings. Shall I go to this restaurant and eat this, or to that restaurant and eat that? At the root of every decision is a preference. Preferences are based on feelings or emotions. Emotions/feelings are directive. They are sometimes subtle but all pervasive. They are within our make-up as persons and clearly part of every decision.

Playing on youngsters' preferences, Shoda, Mischel and Peake (1990) observed preschoolers. They had a choice of eating one marshmallow that was immediately in front of them or wait for two marshmallows. They followed these preschoolers into their teens and reexamined them in other areas of their lives. They found that "cognitive and academic competence and ability to cope with frustration and stress in adolescence" was significantly better for those students who were able to wait and delay their gratification as youngsters (p. 978). Other studies investigating self-regulation indicated that meaningful distraction diverted attention from the temptation that one wanted to avoid. Peake, Helb and Mischel (2002) designed a study that included tasks for participants as well as wait time. This study demonstrated that "attention absorption and self-distraction of the work activity itself appears to be largely responsible for longer delays associated with engaging tasks" (p. 325). So that the more interesting the distracting task is seen, the greater the wait time. The value or meaning of a task is individual. If an individual greatly values a certain task, it will demand attention, and draw the mind away from something of lesser value. This can be used to our advantage. McGonigal (2012) suggested that if we take time to focus on what has the greatest value and provides real rewards, we might be able to use that information to direct our attention away from what really only offers false rewards. Desiring and valuing that which is good for us, directs our actions, and will develop greater self-regulation. Further studies indicated the importance of early self-regulation and the ability to do so was associated with later success in work and relationships. Interest, preferences, and self-regulation seemed to be intertwined. It was also noted that those not able to self-regulate, were not as successful in creating and maintaining relationships.

With the many disturbing violent school incidents, increasing stress levels, bullying issues, and a host of world-wide conflicts including the unsettling and unpredictable terrorist attacks, serious discussions of nurturing emotional intelligence were welcomed by the educational community. Dimensions of emotional maturity were defined and identified. A successful person who could manage social relationships clearly interacted in a manner that was positive for him/her and for the other. Goleman (1995), crediting

Mayer and Salovey for their early work on emotions, created a model that included five dimensions of emotional intelligence:

1. Emotional self-awareness
2. Managing emotions
3. Harnessing emotions productively
4. Empathy
5. Handling relationships

Mayer (2001), similarly, identified emotional maturity or intelligence as the ability to perceive one's own and others' emotions, to access past and present emotions, to understand and manage one's emotions, and to create better and deeper relationships.

Both Goleman's and Mayer's models overlapped with Richburg & Fletcher's (2002) model. Their five domains of emotional intelligence include knowing one's emotion, managing emotions, motivating oneself, recognizing emotions in others, and handling relationships. Self-awareness and management are essential as first steps in the development of emotional intelligence.

Research (Goleman, 1995; Mayor, 2001) in emotional intelligence demonstrated that skills can be learned. Emotions, which are innate, can be positively fostered. They can also be hindered in development. Goleman (1995) reported on several abused children and their behavior toward other children. Kate, 28 months old, knocked a smaller infant to the ground and started with a pat that led to pounding and finally kicking him. Such violence at an early age is considered abnormal. The stories of abused children are repeated as they relate to others. Their emotions have been highjacked. They neither trust nor know how to act appropriately. The natural development of emotions has been stymied.

Goleman (1995) suggested that emotions emerged from basic survival needs. He said emotions evolved as the limbic system developed just near and above the brain stem. An aversive smell of a predator activated the organism's defense system but a familiar, pleasant odor moved the organism toward the source. Survival for simple to complex organisms depends on two basic movements, avoidance and advance. We move towards something because we want it. We move away from something because we determine we do not want it. Advance and retreat are seen as advantageous. Danger or threat is something organisms avoid. Basic research on animals examined reactions as researchers threatened or placed the animal in danger. Rats, for instance, were subjected to shocks. Researchers observed behavior and described strategies that the rats developed in order to avoid danger. Positive experiences, such as the reward of food, were also observed. Brain activation sites followed in the research. Movement toward or away from rewards and punishments were easily identified in animals. While researchers sometimes ascribed feelings to animals (fear of the shock), others carefully avoided such language. In advancing the study of emotions, it was suggested that this two movement survival strategy, advance and retreat in humans, evolved and became associated with particular emotions and feelings. As humans experienced dangerous situations, the feeling of fear emerged. The human brain's alarm system gradually elicited the sense of fear. Likewise, if an advance were made, such as reaching for chocolate cake, pleasure became associated with it. As with the initial animal research, human brain associations and functions were identified with particular tasks or outcomes of various experiments. Early studies were quick to associate the limbic system with emotions (LeDoux, 1998). With increased technology, discrete areas of the brain were associated with specific functions. Eventually, a defense system and a reward system were associated with specific neuronal networks. LeDoux (2012) found the defense reactions system activated particular brain locations. Aversive smells "are detected by the vomeronasal olfactory system and sent to the medial amygdala (MEA), which connects with the verntromedial hypothalamus (VMH). Outputs from the latter reach the premammillary nucleus

(PMH) of the hypothalamus, which connects with dorsal periaque-
ductal gray (PAGd)." Other sensory threats "travel to the lateral
amygdala (LA) and from there to the accessory basal amygdala
(ABA), which connects with the VMH-PM-PAGv circuitry" (p.
656). His research also identified a set of small neurons that communicate from the thalamus directly to the amygdala. The defense
system is triggered when we are conscious of fear but also when we
are unconscious of fear, such as when we step into a crowded New
York subway and there is nowhere to place your hand to hold as the
subway makes a dart for the next station. We may not be conscious
that our hands begin to sweat, but the body's reactions are set in
motion. However, it is only when we are conscious of danger or
threat, that humans experience the sense of fear.

What do humans consider fearful or threatening? If it causes
stress, it is suspicious. Seaward (2002) described three main
sources of stress: *Bioecological* influences remove are external and
can include solar radiation, noise pollution, food additives, seasonal
affect disorders; *Psychintrapersonal* influences (internal) are stimuli that we create through thoughts, values, beliefs, attitudes, per-
ceptions, (used to defend our identity or ego); and *Social influences*, include overcrowding, violation of human rights, and financial insecurity. Sapolsky (1998) remarked that stress in the good
old days meant running from a dangerous animal; today, while the
same bodily reactions occur, we might only minimally be able to
react physically, such as when someone insults us or when we are
barraged by noise pollution, or when we worry about our finances.
Sapolsky wrote, "When we sit around and worry about stressful
things, we turn on the same physiological responses—but they are
potentially a disaster when provoked chronically" (p. 6). The brain
and the body are one and so the whole defense system reacts. In a
stressful situation, the nervous system has the capacity to act in
milliseconds. The sympathetic nervous system prepares the body
for fright, fight, and flight. Heart rate increases, heart contraction

increases, blood glucose levels increase, respiratory rate increases providing greater amounts of oxygen, blood increases to the liver to make more sugars, blood increases to the heart, blood increases to the skeletal muscles, pupils may dilate, and the medulla of adrenals release epinephrine and norepinephrine. Simultaneously, the parasympathetic system is activated and can be evidenced as the GI tract slows down, (Seaward, 2002; McGonigal, 2012). The slightly slower but longer lasting endocrine system responds to stressful stimuli by increasing cortisol levels. This is a cascading event that triggers the several steps. "Information received into the body will make its way to the thalamus. The thalamus will direct the information to other parts of the body. If the information is stress related the thalamus, alerted by the amygdala will send a stress message to the hypothalamus, which activates hormones sent to the pituitary gland. The pituitary secretion of adrenocorticotropin (ACTH) activates the adrenals and in turn releases cortisol. The cortisol is then picked up by the blood stream" (Jensen, 2009). The activation of the hypothalamus, pituitary, and adrenals is called the HPA axis. Hormones in this system can be released throughout the body within eight seconds. Cortisol, which readies us for action, is the main hormone involved in responding to stressful stimuli. This hormone will continue to be released unless otherwise instructed. A person who is under stress, financially or otherwise, may have set the physiological defense system in motion and it may remain that way until the stress is lifted. An animal that runs when frightened uses the energy provided by the defense system as it runs. Humans, faced with psychological stress, fearful or worrisome financial thoughts, do not require the fight or flight response but the body's defense system reacts. Cortisol is released and builds up in the body. Long-term steady release of cortisol destroys the neurons in the hippocampus (Sapolsky, 1998). The hippocampus is essential for episodic memory. Long-term stress, therefore, in humans negatively affects memory. Further, Beilock (2010) reported that stress and worry deplete resources that are needed for working memory and good judgment. She wrote, "Holding on to thoughts and worries under stress leads to an inability to perform the tasks you are faced with" (p. 165). Not only do you not perform as you might but there are actual brain changes. Expert brain activity is different from beginners for the same task. Beginner brains are much more active and in more areas. When some experts are under much stress, their brain activity changes so that the brain activation appears as a beginner's brain (p. 198). Stress compromises working memory. Stress, ultimately will hurt performance (Beilock, 2010, p. 226). Willis (2006) explained that over-activation of the amygdala, produced by stress, will block any new sensory information from entering memory storage.

Goleman (1995) gives an account in his own life of how stress affected performance. He described a moment when his mind went completely blank as he started to take a test. He froze and wasn't able to perform. Beilock (2010) described a time in her life when she too fell short of her normal performance. College recruiters came specifically to watch her as she defended the post in a high school soccer game. She gave her account of how she "choked" and blew the chance she had at one of her dreams. The recruiters went home alone and she went on to college without a soccer scholarship. Beilock spent a great deal of her professional life trying to understand what it is that makes people choke under pressure. She found that those who generally perform better on academic tasks and have strong abilities in problem solving, reasoning, and reading comprehension are most likely to fail under pressure (p. 136). She explained that worries flood the brain and deplete energy needed for performance. Higher levels of cortisol were also associated with poor performance under pressure. She wrote, "Being under pressure alters how different areas of the brain communicate" (p. 153). Neuronal communication systems between pre-frontal and other parts of the brain seem to fail under pressure. Meaney and colleagues (2008, 2012a, 2012b, 2013a, and 2013b) consistently found that glucocorticoid receptors of the hippocampus were associated with stress responses. The more receptors, the lower the hypothalamic pituitary adrenal axis (HPA-endocrine gland interaction) response was to stress. Recall that the HPA axis determines the amount of cortisol released into the blood stream. In animal studies involving rates, heredity influenced the number of receptors, but maternal care increased the number of receptors expressed at the hippocampus. The greater the quality of maternal care the more receptors were present. More receptors mean less cortisol. Animal studies provided the impetus to observe humans. Meany examined brains of those who died from suicide and found that lower numbers of these receptors were found in the brains of those people who were abused and had committed suicide. Meaney and colleagues very clearly identified that negative and positive environmental influences had physical ramifications for brain structure and function.

Davidson (2013) recounts some of his findings in observing negative emotions and brain activation. He and his colleagues showed news clips of tragic events, such as a mining accident and leg amputations. In these experiments, adults' brains were activated in the right prefrontal cortex. He wrote, "Watching clips rated as inducing strong negative emotions while showing expressions of fear or disgust activated the right prefrontal region" (p. 30). He continued his work with infants and children showing them clips of people crying. Babies would be distressed and sometime cry along with the video clip. Other experiments, parent abandonment, the taste of lemon water, and Robbie the Robot all confirmed his earlier findings. The right prefrontal cortex was activated when sad, fearful, or distasteful emotions were aroused. Not only was the limbic system associated with emotions but, now, Davidson and colleagues clearly implicated the right prefrontal cortex with so called negative emotions. People with depression also exhibited higher activity in the right prefrontal cortex. Robbie the Robot experiment had multiple implications. Toddlers who were shy or fearful of the robot also had higher right brain activation but several years later, at age 7 and 9, some of these same toddlers had brain changes. One third of the participants who were shy stayed that way. Two-thirds of the toddlers had switched from either being shy with less right brain activation or switched from being outgoing to the shy continuum with more right brain activation. Davidson examined family experiences and suggested that environmental factors influenced brain changes. Experiences change the brain.

When frightened, a person's defense system triggers a reaction or response that is actualized. Generally it is actualized by three possibilities. Flight, freeze, and fight are the common reactions. Fear then is associated with the response of fighting or what would typically be called aggression or anger. The various nuances and violent expressions of anger, however, cannot be justified as simple reaction/response to a fearful situation or stimulus. The United States Department of Justice for a five-year period (1998–2002) reported more than 32 million violent crimes in the United States, not including murder. Thurman (2005) suggested that anger was "respected as a male prerogative and a privilege of authority" (p. 17). Anger, he says, "when bound with hate overwhelms the reasonable person with a painful vice-grip and uses him or her as a slave" (p. 9). There is evidence that the person who ruminates angrily pays a cost. Denson (2012) after reviewing research in the realm of anger and rumination concluded that "Angry rumination reliably increases aggressive behavior" (p. 113), "can deplete executive control" (p. 112), is related to increased blood pressure, and that angry rumination is "associated with slower cardiovascular and cortisol recovery to baseline levels" (p. 110).

Denson et al., (2008) described two types of aggressive personality dimensions, general aggression (frequent anger and direct retaliation—intense anger and impulsive aggression) and displaced aggression (rumination instead of immediate aggression) (p. 736). Participants in Denson's study completed a series of questionnaires and they were categorized by type of aggression. Participants were then later insulted and associated brain scans were recorded. The results of this study indicated that general anger was associated with greater activity in the dorsal anterior cingulated cortex (dACC), particularly the left, while displaced aggression activated the medial prefrontal cortex (mPFC) to a greater degree (p. 742). General aggression does not necessarily require memory but displaced anger does. In displaced anger the person reviews the event over and over. When a person replays the event, memory is activated. When memory was required as when one ruminates as in displaced anger, then the hippocampus was also active. They also noted that angry rumination increases aggression over time and can lead to violence towards the innocent.

Denson et al. (2012) reviewed many studies and reported that the brain areas that are associated with angry rumination are those associated with cognitive control and emotional regulations. "The neural correlates of provocation and self-focused rumination" were the dorsal anterior cingulate cortex (cognitive control), lateral prefrontal cortex (emotional regulation) the thalamus, amygdala, and insula (arousal) and dorsal medial prefrontal cortex (self-referencing) (p. 107). "Lesions in the orbitofrontal cortex are associated with poor self-regulations," including aggression, so it is likely that this area assists in anger control (p. 108). It may be possible from these studies to identify neurologically those who are prone to aggression and intervene with treatment. Caution is certainly needed as Davidson (2013) described the hunt for the chromosome and gene of the impulsive, aggressive criminal. In 1993 a report on 14 members of an extended family who committed crime revealed an identical form of a gene on the X chromosome. The gene produced an enzyme called MAOA. There are two forms of the enzyme, one that is a short form and one that is a long form. This enzyme that has the shorter form interacts with neurotransmitters in a negative way. Former studies using animals that had a short form of the enzyme appeared to be a factor in aggression. These animal findings propelled the examinations of this gene and enzyme in humans. The investigation of the criminals all within the one family were a prime target for investigating MAOA enzyme. All 14 family members had the short form of MAOA. Interpretations and conclusions in early brain studies require caution. A hasty conclusion to an MAOA enzyme was not in order without further investigations. A study of a large group of New Zealander inmates revealed that criminals tested for the gene had more long forms than short forms of the MAOA type (p. 95–96). MAOA enzyme and its relationship to aggression is presently an active area of research. While the search continues for gene related functions, it is important to balance purely genetic research with environmental interactions. Recall that the research of Meaney et al. (2008, 2012a, 2012b, 2013a, 2013b), and Davidson (2013) gave amble evidenced of environmental effects on brain changes. Studying brain regions and function alone is not enough. Human experiences that change brain structures and functions are needed in the equation.

Negative and positive emotions, while in different areas, were associated with activation of the frontal cortex (Davidson, 2013). The frontal cortex that was typically assigned to tasks such as reasoning, planning, and goal setting is now found to be within some of the same locations associated with emotions. No longer is the frontal cortex considered for higher functioning skills that are disconnected with emotions. It appears that the intellect and emotions are integrally related, both structurally and functionally, in making healthy decision. Shiv and Nowlis (2004) described a two-component model for making a choice or decision, an affective component and an informational component. They found that both components working together are necessary for experiencing the greatest pleasure in tasting food. They wrote, "Ultimate pleasure arising from the taste of a food sample depends on two components, one informational and the other affective" (p. 599).

Berridage and Kringelbach (2013) distinguished three components of the reward system: liking, wanting, and reward related learning. Each component has a unique response in the brain. The reward system can be triggered in association with a conscious sense of pleasant feelings but also can be triggered when not aware as unconscious pleasure. Good feeling neurotransmitters are also implicated in the reward system. Dopamine was one of the first to be associated with the reward system. With discrete tasks and better imaging techniques, dopamine is better associated with the wanting component of the reward system. Dopamine is associated with motivation or anticipation of the reward. It's the stuff that gets you moving towards the pleasurable goal. The liking component is better associated with endogenous opioid and endocannabinoid. "Opioid and endocannabinoid neurochemical signals do more effectively generate intense pleasures than dopamine" (p. 299). The brain regions or "hot spots" for opioid and endocannabinoid are the nucleus accumbens circuitry (NAc) and the posterior half of the ventral pallidum. "Functionally, hotspots in the NAc and ventral pallidum interact together in a single integrated circuit" (p. 299). Lesions in these two areas dampen any sense of pleasure. The amygdala has generally been associated with all emotions but studies indicate that it is not associated with happiness, per se, but with the anticipation or wanting component of the reward system. The orbitofrontal cortex is associated with affective regulation, the reward related learning which is the third component of the reward system (Berridage et al., 2013).

Davidson's (2013) neuroimaging data specified brain areas for positive emotions. Clips of *The Carol Burnett Show* were shown to adult participants. These experiments revealed that adult brains were activated in the left prefrontal cortex, just the opposite of the negative emotion brain sites. In his studies with infants and children, he showed them clips of people laughing. Spontaneously, toddlers would smile and giggle. He used sugar water instead of lemon water. Here too, the left side of the brain was activated. Toddlers who interacted positively with Robbie the Robot also confirmed the left brain activation site. Davidson, in capturing true smiles, while at the same time using brain scans, found activation of the left side of the frontal brain. Positive emotions, Davidson concluded are associated with activation of the left side of the prefrontal brain. A simple simile will activate this side of the brain.

McGonigal's (2012), research and review of research supported an interacting system of intellect and emotions. She said that will power is the ability to control attention, emotions, and desires. Will power, which attends to the affective and the intellect, determines life's choices (p. 1). She indicated that will power consists of three components: I want, I will, and I won't; each one is associated with activation in the frontal cortex. The successful management of our will power, she said, is a universal struggle and understanding what comprises this struggle will be influential in controlling our impulses and make for better decision making. Will power is at the crossroads of emotions and intellect. The ability to control our will power affects relationships, health, wealth, and success in life. Will power gives us the ability to self-regulate. The good news, McGonigal's research indicated, will power can be increased. She identified the frontal lobe for the three locations. "I will" is associated with the left side; "I won't" is associated with the right side. "I want" was found to be activated in the central part of the frontal lobe (p. 13). So how can we resist that chocolate or do that tedious job? How can we control our impulses and increase the ability to self-regulate? How can we make this world a better place for ourselves and others? Recall that Phineas Gage had these abilities and lost self-regulation through the accident that destroyed part of the frontal lobe. The frontal lobe communicating with other parts of the brain is essential for emotional well-being. Beilock (2010) wrote

"Despite innate differences, our eventual level of success is mark-edly affected by training and practice" (p. 49). This is not only the case when dealing with stress but in increasing self-regulation and emotional control. McGonigal's (2012) book offered multiple true and tried strategies. She found that over-load of daily will power exercises will deplete your ability to be successful. Willis (2006) also reported that neurotransmitters can be depleted in overtaxing situations. McGonigal recommended that strategies be used pur-posely. Start with simple tasks. Will power exercises, used over the long-term, will increase skills, even if there are daily downfalls. Self-awareness is the first essential in will power. As previously noted in emotional intelligence models, self-awareness is the first essential. Stop to reflect. When and what are your will power chal-lenges? What time of day are you most successful? When the least? McGonigal reminded the reader that as the day wears on, so too, does our ability to use will power, because using will power is similar to using a muscle. If used properly, the skill is developed. If used too much, physical energy will actually be depleted. Practice small but consistent exercises. Give yourself a rule for your greatest challenge, such as, drink water and wait ten minutes before diving into the ice cream. There are many versions of the breathing exer-cise. Consistent use of this kind of focus activity increases will power and also shows structural benefits in the brain, increased gray and white matter. Increased will power abilities in one area will affect other areas of your life. Finkel, Slotter, DeWall and Oaten (2009), suggested, through their research, "that individuals perpetrate intimate partner violence because society socializes them to do so" (p. 483). They found that if "self-regulatory resources were bolstered" through the use of their two week training model, then positive outcomes for partner relationships emerged (p. 483). Partners had better control and better interactions with one another. McGonigal (2012), wrote, "People who have better control of their attention, emotions, and actions are better off almost any way you

look at it"; they are happier, healthier, have longer-lasting relationships, make more money, manage stress better, overcome adver-
sity, are academically more successful and live longer (p. 12).
Emotions are at the heart of decision-making and well-being.

Educational Connections

Emotions direct our every decision. The first step in managing
emotions is self-awareness. Skills related to emotional intelligence
can be learned. Practicing exercises to build will power increases
self-regulation. Over-exercising will power or self-regulation de-
pletes resources and back-fires. Consistent practice over the long
term will increase will power and self-regulation skills.

Experiences change structure and functionality of the brain.
Overly stressful environments have a negative effect on learning.
Cortisol levels are elevated in anxious or stressful situation. Environments that are stressful over a long period of time will have
physical implications for the brain. Consistent increased levels of
cortisol will destroy neurons in the hippocampus. The hippocampus
is the brain's filing system. Eliminating unnecessary stress increases the ability to learn. Where stress is unavoidable, practicing
in a similarly stressful situation, will improve performance. Angry
rumination increases the likelihood of violence to the innocent.
Both stress and anger deplete executive function and working
memory. Positive environments have physiological implications
for learning. Providing positive education experiences that connect
with emotions develops emotional intelligence. Positive emotional
experiences can change brain structure and functionality. Willis
(2006) reported that positive working environments increased
working memory, verbal fluency, episodic memory, problem solving, and creativity (p. 24).

Questions to consider:

How do your lesson plans include emotions?

What in your curriculum addresses self-awareness?

How informed are you about the dimensions of emotional intelligence?

How is each dimension developed in the curriculum?

Are plans inclusive of developing emotional vocabulary?

What easy but consistent practices are provided for self-regulation?

Do you include breathing exercises or five minutes of quiet observations?

Is the daily schedule overtaxing thereby depleting brain power?

What unnecessary stress can be eliminated from daily, weekly, yearly schedules?

If stress cannot be eliminated, what helps are given to encourage peak performance?

What is provided to develop skills to manage anger?

How can you restructure the environment to increase positive experiences?

Do you know what students enjoy?

Is there a way to increase your knowledge of students' interests?

Examine each of the teaching disciplines and establish connections with local resources. There are many local opportunities that connect the emotions with learning. Two examples in the arts discipline in the Maryland area include:

1. The Walters Arts Museum provides a free Saturday experience. Children's activities are provided that artistically explore works of art and make connections with exhibits. Past activities included crafts such as dragon making, patterns and prints, clay creations, carved boxes and interactive art.

2. Pumpkin Theatre was established to entertain, educate and delight children. The theatre produces fairy tales and folk tales throughout the year. In addition to performances for the general public, Pumpkin Theatre designed Pathways for ele-

mentary students. Older children can attend drama and musical theatre classes. Involving a child emotionally, socially
and intellectually enhances the ability to learn.

How can you connect with outside sources such as these?

Chapter Four

Social and Moral Perspectives

We are social beings and so it is natural for us to communicate and interact in many ways and on different levels with one another. Oral language is a major form of communication. It is an expression of who we are, what we need, and desire. Language emerges only within a community. In communities throughout the world, language follows a universal pattern of development. Babbling is the first spontaneous stage. All sounds are babbled. An attentive mother engages with her infant in babbling. Goleman (2006) reported that the adult complement of baby talk always sounds "friendly and playful with a high pitch" at 300 hertz (p. 36). "Mother and infant fall into what seems much like a duet of synchronized or alternating parts, paced by a steady adagio pulse at about 90 beats per minute" (p. 36). The mother encourages the infant's cooing and movement of tongue, lip, and jaws (p. 36). The practice of babbling and forms of vocalization prepare the necessary muscles for fine control. McWhorter (2012) noted that while all sounds are babbled, there seems to be an order in which they are perceived. The *b* and *d* sounds are first to be perceived and first to be voiced. They are referred to as voiced stops. The nasals are perceived next (e.g. *m* sound). The short a sound is one of the first vowel sounds to be spoken. The fricatives and liquids, *l, r, y s, v, z* sounds, are among the last to be voiced along with the consonant sounds of *sh,* *ch, ng, zh,* and *th*. It is not unusual to hear *dat* for that. Typically by age two, all consonant sounds, except versions of the *j,* can be reproduced. Individual sounds, called phonemes, eventually provide the basis to imitate and make use of single words. In the initial use of words, children will make substitutions using the more common sounds for those less practiced sounds, such as using *ting* for *sing*, and *doe* for *go*. By age one and a half, toddlers know about 50 words. Grasping the full meaning of the words takes longer. For instance, learning a new word, such as dog, children may refer to any four-legged creature as dog. This is called overextension of a word. Underextension is also common; a child will learn a particular word but fail to extend it to other objects, such as the dog sits but sit might not be connected to anything else. As children grow older, so their vocabulary develops and so, too, the proper understanding and usage of words. There is a natural decline in such errors as overextension and underextension.

Not only language, but also the structure or morphology of a language is largely assimilated through informal interactions. Early on, children will correctly use the word feet for the plural of foot because they carefully imitate adults, but as they progress, the rules of grammar become implicitly known. They learn that the simple rule for plurals is to add an *s*. Now that they know the rule for plurals, instead of using the correct form as they did, they will say foots for the plural of foot and mans, instead of men. When children use gooses instead of geese or foots instead of feet, they are extending the rules of grammar. It is referred to as overgeneralization of the rule or over-regularization. Exceptions to the rules of the English language and other languages are learned later. Body parts are recognized between two and three years of age. One word usage develops into the use of sentences. Sentences emerge by age two and a half and children easily communicate ideas such as "I want teddy." The use of articles, however, is generally not present at this age. By age three or four, sentences may include four or five words and children know about 1000 words. At this age, they will begin to use past tense; they recognize that time has past and there will be a tomorrow. At about age five, children are learning up to 20 words a day and have a 10,000-word vocabulary (Lighbown & Spada, 2006, McWhorter, 2012). Language now provides a world of connections and an ability to share with others. Cozolino (2013) wrote that language was the vehicle that allowed for complex social interactions, understanding the minds of others, and giving meaning to narratives. Language is social.

Vygotsky (1978) proposed that language develops in the presence of others, within a particular community. In fact, all learning reflects the social and cultural environment. Tragic stories of feral children, not wanted by their parents, support Vygotsky's theory of social cultural learning. One such story is that of Oxana Malaya. At the age of three she crawled into the dogs' cage to keep warm. The dogs were her caregivers to age eight. Her social milieu was that of the world of the dogs. See http://www.youtube.com/watch?v=2PyUfG9u-P4. She barked and howled instead of speaking. These cases are extreme and jolting in the lessons that they teach us.

In normal settings, research supports the need for human interaction. While biology matters, Stolt, Korja, Matomaki, Lapinleimu, Haataja, and Lehtonen (2014) found that the mothers' interactions with babbling infants influenced language development. Goleman (2006) suggested that interaction of mother and infant not only assist in language development but also social interaction. He stated, "the protoconversation marks a baby's first lesson in how to interact" (p. 37). Bannard and Klinger (2013) found that three-year-olds use imitation of new vocabulary words in two ways, blind imitation and insightful imitation. Blind imitation was found to be a necessary part of vocabulary development. In blind imitation, toddlers repeated words mechanically without understanding, so toddlers used words even when there was no communicative motivation (p. 2353). Insightful imitations indicate understanding of a concept, in this case toddlers would use a word correctly and for meaning. When words had meaning, toddlers used them more. Rakoczy, Hamann, Warneken and Tomasello (2010) found that, by age two, children imitated adults using objects in the correct manner and generally prefer to learn from adults rather than peers. Children also enforced rules for game playing, as they had learned them from adults. By age two, they also knew agent intention and were able to decide who was reliable. They would choose to imitate the reliable agent over the unreliable agent (one that made mistakes). Tomasellso, Carpenter, Call, Behne and Moll (2005) stated that humans are experts in mind reading and that language requires the ability to read the intentions of others. One movement might mean "giving an object, sharing it, loaning it, moving it, getting rid of it, returning it, trading it, selling it . . . depending on the goal and intention of the actor" (p. 675). A child of one year has the ability to do this. Further, the authors indicated that humans have the ability to have "shared intentionality" (p. 676) and that this develops as early as 14 months. In other words, toddlers interact with others in a way that shows they understand the intentions of the other. Language establishes connections with the other.

Rizzolatti and Craighero (2004) wrote, "we are able to learn by imitation, and this faculty is at the basis of human culture" (p. 169). Their research focuses on the mirror neuron system. The function of mirror neurons, they explained, is to mediate imitation and to understand intentions and actions of others. Mirror neurons are neurons that activate in one person who observes another person. The same area of the brain that is required for the one is activated in the other. So if George watches Mary grasping for a glass of water, the brain activation in Mary that needed to grasp for the glass will activate the same brain area in George as he observes. The difference is that George will not do the action because "in the spinal cord, there is an inhibitory mechanism that prevents the execution of an observed action, thus leaving the cortical motor system free to 'react' to the action without the risk of overt movement generation" (p. 175). The mirror neurons have been observed in all of the lobes of the brain. The core of the mirror system, however, is particularly regulated in the "inferior parietal lobule, the lower part of the pre-central gyrus, and the posterior part of the inferior frontal gyrus" (p. 176). An observer's frontal lobe will activate when watching the hand and arm movements of another. The precentral gyrus and the posterior parietal lobe will activate when we observe a foot or leg actions of another. When observing another's intentions to use se-quential movements, the observer activated the frontal mirror-neuron system. Nishitani and Hari (2002) stated, "Viewing other persons' actions automatically activates brain areas belonging to the mirror-neuron system" (p. 1211). Their study involved partici-pants observing lip formation and imitating the lip formation that they observed. Activation of neurons were observed first in the occipital lobe, next in superior temporal, which then activated the inferior parietal, and finally to the fronto-central in each hemi-sphere (motor cortex). In both observation and imitation, the same brain sites were activated. The authors proposed that there was a mirror neuron speech evolution. They suggested that the Broca's area "has played a crucial role in the evolution of the gestural basis for language and speech" (p. 1217). Speech evolution emerged from hand gestures to symbolic sounds. Rizzolatti and Craighero (2004) also suggested that the activation of early gestural neurons evolved to include mirror neurons used in communication. Mirror neurons connect us with the other. We experience the other and can read their intentions. Zwickel, White, Coniston, Senju and Frith (2011) stated that "human interaction depends on the ability to attribute mental states to other agents" (p. 564). Mirror neurons predispose us to do just that.

Experiencing the other is at the root of empathy. Fan, Duncan, de Greck, and Northoff (2011) make a distinction among the concepts of sympathy, theory of mind, emotional contagion, and empathy. Sympathy and theory of mind are considered distinct from empathy in that they demonstrate understanding but no sharing of another's state. Emotional contagion differs from empathy, in that it lacks awareness as to the source of the experienced state. Empathy requires awareness, understanding, and sharing of another's state (p. 904). Schnell, Bluschke, Konradt and Walter (2011) further described two components of empathy, affective and cognitive or "mentalizing." Cognitive empathy or mentalizing is the ability to make inferences about the mental state of others. In examining the brain areas for both affective and cognitive empathy, Fan et al. (2011) identified the dorsal anterior cingulate cortex dACC, anterior med-cingulate cortex, (aMCC), supplementary motor area (SMA), and the bilateral anterior insula as active. They were also able to distinguish the cognitive forms of empathy as associated with aMCC while the affective form activated the right anterior insula. The left anterior insula was active in both forms of empathy. Additional areas that have been associated with mentalizing are the dorsomedial prefrontal cortex (dmPFC), superior temporal sulcus (STS), the temporo-parietal junction (TPJ), and the anterior temporal poles (TP). The limbic system, particularly the amygdala and hippocampus are active in affective processing of emotions. The hippocampus may be activated if context is needed for understanding (Schnell, Bluschke, Konradt and Walter, 2011).

Singer and Frith (2005) wondered how someone could know how it feels for another to be in pain. Their research supports that observations of another in pain automatically activates the neuronal network that is processed as though the observer were experiencing the pain first hand. The neural substrates of social and physical pain are of two types, a sensory experience that detects where, what kind, and how much pain, registered in the somatosensory cortex and an affective component of pain registered in the anterior cingulate cortex (locates pain sensation) (BA 24, 32) and the anterior insula (registers the distress) (Eisenberger, 2012, 2013). These areas are activated when experiencing pain first hand or observing another. Singer and Frith (2005) noted that the amount of activation in these sites when observing others in pain varied. They suggested that the "key variable is likely to be the mental attitude of the participants when thinking about the pain of others" (p. 846). In other words, some people are more sensitive in sensing the pain of others. Eisenberger (2012) reportedly examined social rejection because of her own experience of pain through peer rejection. She wrote, "Some of the most distressing experiences that we face involve the dissolution of our closest social bonds" (p. 421). These experiences have been described as being painful. Her colleague, Jarcho, was researching physical pain and reviewing the data from neuroimaging studies. As officemates they compared notes. The same areas of the brain that were activated for physical pain were found to be the locations for social rejection. Further studies demonstrated that taking pain medicine for physical pain had a similar effect for relieving social pain. The evolutionary process in the development of brain areas associated with physical pain emerged also as the associated area for pain of social rejection. Eisenberger (2012) wrote "the social attachment system may have piggybacked onto the opiod substrates of the physical pain system" for comfort and ease of pain (p. 422). Opiates are mediated by the OPMR1 gene. The opioid system relieves pain, physical and social, and increases pleasure associated with social connection. Perceived social dissociation increases the likelihood of inflammation, of heart disease, and depression. Greater risk for mortality is associated with those who are isolated (Eisenberger, 2012).

The ability to be socially connected came from our need to survive. We do better as a group in protecting ourselves from the predator. Maintaining ties as a group is work. Goleman (2006) outlined what is required for *social intelligence*. He said there are two broad categories, social awareness and social facility. To be socially aware means that one is able to feel with others, sensing non-verbal communication; it means one is able to listen to the other, attune to the person; it means we are capable of understanding another person's thoughts, feelings and intentions; it requires that one knows how the social world works. He called these four elements of *social awareness* primal empathy, attunement, empathic accuracy, and social cognition. The second category of social intelligence, *social facility*, is what we do with social awareness. It involves interacting smoothly at the nonverbal level; presenting ourselves effectively; shaping the outcome of social interactions; caring about others' needs and acting accordingly. He called these four elements of social facility as synchrony, self-presentation, influence, and concern (p. 84). He reported that particular cells called spindle cells are four times larger than any other brain cell. Neuroimaging has found thick connections in the orbital frontal lobe and the anterior cingulate cortex. It is suggested that these cells work in concert with social awareness. This is the area where empathy is activated. He stated this neural node is crucial in "our social decision-making" (p. 68). "This circuitry appraises all we experience, assigning value-liking or disliking-and so it shapes our very sense of meaning, of what matters" (p. 68).

As Singer et al. (2005) explained that some people seem to be more sensitive than others in responding to the pain of others, Kohlberg wondered how so many people could allow the systematic killing of the Jewish people to happen during the 1940s. He wondered how so many people could take an active role in this tragic human story. The Jewish Holocaust propelled his moral development theory. Research with infants supports the idea of the quote from *South Pacific*, "You have to be carefully taught to hate." Hamlin and Wynn (2011) investigated infants' preference for either prosocial or antisocial others. Their research objective was to observe infants, five to nine months, evaluating mean or caring puppets. The results supported the stance that "infants positively assess those who aid others" to reach a goal and "negatively assess those who block such goals" (p. 37). Their findings are similar to Hamlin, Wynn and Bloom (2007) who found that infants avoid those who hindered others and approach those who have helped. Hamlin et al. (2011) suggested that infants this age are too young to be socialized toward the tendency to want to interact with the helpful puppet but that it is likely there is a "cognitive mechanism supporting the evolution of our cooperative tendencies" (p. 38). They suggested that there is a natural tendency, perhaps for survival and safety of the group, to select for helpful and prosocial behaviors. See the ABC special highlighting Wynn's research at http://www.youtube.com/watch?v=F-UQkDs9I0I. Societal and cultural influences build on these natural tendencies as Tomasello (2000) stated that children do not learn from adults but "through" adults. They are socialized by understanding another's intention, by knowing "something of the adult's perspective" (p. 39). Hamlin and Wynn (2012), extending their work to 16-month-olds, wrote "Most of what we know comes from others" (p. 227). They found that children are able to distinguish and imitate those "worthy" teachers who have positive intentions from those who are "unworthy" and better to avoid. These infant studies indicate that we are predisposed to be social and cooperative.

Caring and cooperating with others, valuing the other person means that we do no harm. When we act socially intelligent, we care for others. How could things go so wrong if we are predisposed for good? Lieberman (2013) wrote, "Those who had been bullied at age eight were more than six times as likely to have actually taken their own lives by the age of twenty-five" (p. 69). He suggested that rejection is a fate worse than death. Powers, Wagner, Norris and Heatherton (2011) reported that those who were socially excluded and bullied have reduced abilities to care for others in need. While we may be predisposed for cooperation, children imitate and model what they see and experience on a daily bases.

Kohlberg's (1978) research found that we go through stages as we learn to care for and value the other. His moral development theory presented six sequential stages. He suggested that children and adults could be coaxed through various stages. This could be accomplished by challenging their reasoning abilities one stage in advance of their present reasoning skills. He admitted that having the ability to reason at higher levels did not mean that one would act that way but the possibility was greater to act the way. Practice and developing habits of behavior become part of who the person is. (See Table 4.1)

Pre-conventional reasoning is connected with punishment and its avoidance. In interviews with children at age five, it was clear to see they were true to Stage 1 as evidenced by their comments.

Question: Why shouldn't you do bad things? Why shouldn't someone be mean?

Stage 1 Comments:

Mom and Dad will be mad and won't let you go to school anymore

If you will be mean, you will sit on the principal's bench

Table 4.1. Kohlberg's Six Stages of Moral Development (Adapted from Traviss, 1985)

Pre Conventional Level	Stage 1. Punishment and Obedience Orientation	Might makes right
	Stage 2. Instrumental Relativist Orientation	Scratch my back, I'll scratch yours
Conventional Level	Stage 3. Interpersonal Concordance	Good boy, nice girl—approval
	Stage 4. Law and Order Orientation	Fixed rules—right behavior consists in doing one's duty
Post Conventional Level	Stage 5. Social Contract / Legalistic Orientation	Standards critically examined and agreed upon by whole society
	Stage 6. Universal Ethical Principle	Universal justice, equality

If you are mean, you are going to get in a fight and you can't fight—if Jesus sees you,

Jesus is going to punish you.

(If you are mean) Sent to your room

Adults who understand moral development stages can discuss with a child at Stage 1 with Stage 2 reasoning. They can ask questions that will help them to think. If a friend hurts you is s/he a good friend? If you are mean to your friend, will s/he want to be a friend to you? These questions are complementary to Stage 2 reasoning of reciprocity: *If you are nice to me, I will be nice to you.*

Enculturation is ever present. In one particular study, adult participants were presented with words that were either related to rude behavior or to polite behavior. Participants were then placed in a situation with a research compatriot. The interaction that followed between the compatriot and participant was predictable by the earlier presentation of word priming. Those who were primed toward positive words acted as anticipated while those presented with rude words were also predictable in their behavior. Goleman (2006) reported that even when we look upon faces that display strong emotions, such as sadness, disgust, or joy, "our facial muscles automatically start to mirror the other's facial expression" (p. 18). Lieberman (2013) wrote "our brains are designed to be influenced by others" (p. 8). He suggested that we are wired to be social and that social connections are linked to our well-being. Gusnard, Akbudak, Shulman, and Raichle (2001) investigated the brain at rest using fMRI. They found that when the brain is not at work with a task but rather at rest, it is activated more in the medial prefrontal cortex. Areas BA eight, nine and ten are associated with self-referencing. That is when our brains are at rest, the focus of our thoughts are on the self and others. Our default brain mode is to think about our relationships. They noted that a brain at rest is hardly inactive as "The MPFC is also among those brain regions having the highest baseline metabolic activity" (p. 4260). It appears that our favorite brain activity is social and full of personal narratives. Young children have make-believe stories that are real to them. In asking children in the pre-conventional level what they are afraid of, they commented: *Monsters, really bad monsters with one eye and blue monsters really big with three eyes; Afraid of the dark and jolly bees; Giant monster who lives under a rock; it lives there and it is real; Afraid of foot long spiders; Monsters, really mean ones.* It was striking to note the concerns of two children both who mentioned, in separate interviews, that they were very afraid of the same character that they had seen in a movie. The character is vicious, insidious, and successful. A character that should be innocent and safe was transformed into a cruel and monstrous character, feared as real by these young minds. Young minds need characters that are good, true, reliable, and predictable, characters worth imitating.

Children in the conventional stage are very concerned with fairness and treating others fairly. Eight- and nine-year-olds will think it is unfair if someone is left out of a game. If they have two cookies, they want to share one with a friend. You will hear the words: *That's not fair.* Rules are very important at this stage and need to be so. One student commented: *Can't change or break rules, You can't!* It is very important for students to have the time to be in this stage, to realize the importance of keeping rules and treating others fairly and kindly. Empathy and associated brain responses are modulated by one's sense of fairness. Singer, Seymour, O'Doherty, Stephan, Dolan and Frith (2006) provided "neurobiological evidence of how fairness in social interactions shapes the nature of the affective link between people" (p. 467). They further found that when considering the link between empathy and fairness, "that cooperation nourishes this link but selfish behavior, detrimental to others effectively compromises this link (at least in males), such that empathic responses in the brain are diminished or abolished" (p. 467). Empathic responses were activated in the fronto-insular and anterior cingulate cortices when participants perceived fair interactions. In males, unfair interactions activated the revenge circuitry. Both sexes empathized with the social behaviors that were perceived as fair (p. 466). Lieberman (2013) reported that when we perceive that we are being treated fairly our "brain's reward" system is turned on (p. 74). Fairness and our understanding of it change, as our thinking and reasoning skills change. Students about the age of 11 or 12 are ready for the next stage questions, such as, is it ever OK to go through a red light or should stealing always be punished, Questions such as these will encourage students to think about different possibilities, and different motivation. Keeping the rules as designed with no violation of them is typical of the students age seven through ten, but exceptions to rules are examined as issues of fairness require more complicated reasoning skills.

There is no denying the dehumanizing events of history and the cruelty of individuals. Goleman (2006) discussed the "Dark Triad," the narcissist, the Machiavellian, and the psychopath. They have turned off their ability to feel with others or to care about the other. He wrote, "Suppressing our natural inclination to feel with another unleashes cruelty" (p. 117). "Empathy," he said, "is the prime inhibitor of human cruelty" (p. 116). Considering that we are hardwired for cooperation, Goleman reminded his readers that if we evaluate all the evil in light of all the good, humans come out on the side of good. While donations are only one way to show interest and a sense of care for others, it is noteworthy that the United States averages over $300 billion a year to charities (Goleman, 2006). Research indicates that a particular area of the brain activates in relationship to a caring act. In Lieberman's (2013) work involving empathy, he concluded, "the septal area appeared to be a marker of empathic motivation" (p. 157). The septal area has direct connections to the dorsomedial prefrontal cortex, "the CEO of the brain's mentalizing system" (p. 158). The septal area is critical for maternal caregiving, for dampening the feeling of distress, and for experiencing rewards. "We need the septal region . . . to nudge us to actually get involved in the lives of those around us in positive ways" (Lieberman 2013, p. 161). Empathy is required for social intelligence. "Listening with full receptivity" is one of the required elements of social awareness (Goleman, 2006, p. 84). In Norway some schools have been established to teach conflict transformation, which is based on total respect for every person. These are called Sabona Schools, which means, "I see you" in Swahili. To acknowledge the other, to see the other is to say I value you, I see that you are there. Your desires and needs are as important as mine. McCarthy (2008), who after a long career as a journalist for the *Washington Post*, became involved in peace education. He directed the Center for Teaching Peace, in Washington, DC. He found it an uphill battle to incorporate peace education into the schools. McCarthy asked his University students to write a paper on the importance of peace education. He recalled the shortest and most insightful paper he ever received. The student wrote, "Question: Why are we violent but not illiterate. Answer: Because we have been taught to read." Society transmits what it truly values. After providing training in social and emotional skills, Ornaghi, Brock-meier and Grazzani (2014) concluded that training improved "children's cognitive and socioemotional competencies" and these skills remained with them after a follow-up six months later (p. 36). Kohlberg (1978) also realized that training would advance moral reasoning. Vygotsky's concept of the zone of proximal development and learning through role modeling are complementary tools for moral stage development. The last level of Kohlberg's theory is the post-conventional level. At this level justice and equality are the qualities that inform decisions. Gilligan's (1993) research included care of self and others as paramount in moral reasoning and corresponding actions. Lieberman (2013) concluded that "everything we have learned about the social brain tells us that we are wired to make and keep social connections, that we feel pain when these connections are threatened, and that our identity, our sense of self, is intimately tied up with the groups we are a part of" (p. 249).

Educational Connections

Language is learned in a social context. It gives us the ability to interact with one another and express our deepest desires. A serious problem facing us today according to Goleman (2006) is the isolation and disconnection experienced by so many adolescences.

Questions:

> How can schools be built and organized to facilitate connections?
> What in the curriculum allows for student-to-student connections?
> How can these connections be safe?

We are hard wired to cooperate. Lieberman (2013) wrote that helping and connecting with others motivates people to work harder (p. 264). Students who participate in Service Learning activities are helpful and connected. Eyler and Giles (1999) have researched and identified some of the student benefits of service-learning engagements: greater motivation towards course involvement, deeper understanding of course content, general improved learning, enhanced critical thinking and problem-solving, reflective judgment, and social responsibility. Many states have adopted some form of service learning.

Questions:

> How can you provide a meaningful opportunity for students to help others?
> What daily opportunities are provided for cooperation?

Goleman (2006) provides a social intelligence model? Kohlberg (1978) and Gilligan (1999) provide moral development theories. Illinois State Board of Education requires schools to incorporate Social and Emotional Learning Standards for K-12 students. For a copy of standards, go to http://www.isbe.net/ils/social_emotional/standards.htm.

Questions:

> How familiar are teachers with stages of social and moral development?
> How are teachers encouraged to implement a curriculum that reflects social and moral stage development?
> Does the curriculum include standards for student growth in social-emotional development?
> Are lessons inclusive of social and moral development?
> Is there a peace education curriculum available?
> How can faculty help each other in creating an environment that reflects social and moral development?

The default brain system is the self-referencing areas. On our downtime we seriously consider our relationship and personal narratives. Cozolino (2013) suggested that narratives are essential for learning. He said the stories are powerful tools to impact our self-identity. Children "demand that you tell them the same story every night" (p. 189).

Questions:

> Are stories incorporated into lessons?
> How are children able to express themselves through narratives?
> What characters are used to model social interactions?
> How can parents be involved in positive story time?
> Can stories be used to enliven subject material?
> How can stories be used to help students with self-awareness?

How can stories be used to increase social and moral awareness? What stories are included in the curriculum that illustrate great men and women of peace?

References

Amnesia. (2007). Retrieved March 12, 2014, from Neuroslicer, http://www.youtube.com/watch?v=ZHUvCR-2AOcz

Bagot, R. C., & Meaney, M. J. (2010). Epigenetics and the biological basis of gene x environment interactions. *Journal of the American Academy of Child and Adolescent Psychiatry*, 49(8), 752-771. DOI: 10.1016/j.jaac.2010.06.001

Bannard, C., & Klinger, J. (2013). How selective are 3-year-olds in imitating novel linguistic material? *Developmental Psychology*, 49(12), 2344-2356. DOI: 10.1037/a0032062

Batholomew, D. J., Allerhand, M., & Deary, J. (2013). Measuring mental capacity: Thomson's bonds model and Sperarman's g-model compared. *Intelligence*, 41(4), 222-233. DOI: 10.1016/j.intell.2013.03.007

Beilock, S. (2010). *Choke:* What the secrets of the brain reveal about getting it right when you have to. New York, NY: Free Press.

Berridge, K. C., & Kringelbach, M. L. (2013). Neuroscience of affect: Brain mechanisms of pleasure and displeasure. *Current Opinion in Neurobiology*, 23, 294-303. DOI: 10.1093/oxfordhb/9780199570706.013.0018

Blair, C. (2007). R3. Darker conceptual clods-What is "intelligence." Response/ Jung&Haier: Converging neuroimaging evidence. *Behavioral and Brain Sciences*, 30(2) 135-187. DOI: 10.1017/S0140525X07001185.

Carraher, T., Darraher, D., & Schliemann, A. (1985). Mathematics in the streets and in the schools. *British Journal of Developmental Psychology*, 3, 21-29. DOI: 10.1111/j.2044-835X.1985.tb00951.x

Cozolino, L. (2013). *The social neuroscience of education: Optimizing attachment & learning in the classroom.* New York, NY: W. W. Norton & Company, Inc.

Damasio, A. R. (1998). Emotion in the perspective of an integrated nervous system. *Brain Research Review,* 26, 83-86. DOI: 10.1016/S0165-0173(97)00064-7

Davidson, R. J. & Begley, S. (2013). *The emotional life of your brain.* New York, NY: A Plume Book.

Denson, T. F. (2012). The multiple systems model of angry rumination. *Personality and Social Psychology Review*, 17(2), 103-123. DOI: 10.1177/1088868312467086.

Denson, T. F., Pedersen, W. C., Ronquillo, J., & Nandy, A. S. (2008). The angry brain: Neural correlates of anger, angry rumination, and aggressive personality. *Journal of Cognitive Neural Science*, 21(4), 734.744. DOI: 10.1162/jocn.2009.21051

Dodson & Horrell. (2012, September 11). Working Dogs – How dogs herd sheep. Retrieved February 28, 2014, from http://www.dodsonandhorrellpetfood.co.uk/blog/dogs-2/working-dogs-how-dogs-heard-sheep/

Dubin, M. (2009). Brodmann Areas in the Human Brain with an Emphasis on Vision and Language. Retrieved March 12, 2014, from University of Colorado, http://spot.colorado.edu/~dubin/talks/brodmann/brodmann.html

Ebbinghaus, H. (1885/1913). *Concerning Memory.* (H.A. Ruger and C. E. Bussenius, Trans.). Columbia University, NY: Teachers College.

———. (1885/1913). *Learning and Retention: Experiments in Memory.* (H.A. Ruger and C. E. Bussenius, Trans.). Columbia University, NY: Teachers College.

———. (1885/1913). *Retention as a Function of the Number of Repetitions.* (H.A. Ruger and C. E. Bussenius, Trans.). Columbia University, NY: Teachers College.

Eisenberger, N. (2012). The pain of social disconnection: Examining the shared neural underpinnings of physical and social pain. *Nature Reviews. Neuroscience*, 13(6), 421-434. DOI: 10.1038/nrn3231

———. (2013). An empirical review of the neural underpinnings of receiving and giving social support: *Implications for health. Psychosomatic Medicine*, 75(6), 545-556. DOI: 10.1097/psy.0b013e31829de2e7

Ekman, P. (2003). *Emotions revealed: Recognizing faces and feelings to improve communication and emotional life.* New York, NY: Henry Holt and Company.

Eyler, J. & Giles, D. E. (1999). *Where's the learning in service-learning?* San Francisco. CA: Jossey-Bass Publishers.

Fan, Y., Duncan, N. W., de Greck, M., & Northoff, G. (2011). Is there a core neural network in empathy? An fMRI based quantitative meta-analysis. *Neuroscience and Biobehavioral Review*, 35, 903-911. DOI: 10.1016/j.neubiorev.2010.10.009

Finkel, E. J., Slotter, E. B., DeWall, C. N., & Oaten, M. (2009). Self-regulatory failure and intimate partner violence perpetration. *Journal of Personality and Social Psychology*, 97(3), 483-499. DOI: 10.1037/a0015433

Fleischman, J. (2002). *Phineas Gage: A gruesome but true story about brain science.* Boston, MA: Houghton Mifflin Company.

Gardner, H. (2011). *Multiple Intelligence: New horizons.* New York, NY: Basic Books.

Gazzaniga, M. S., Ivry, R. B., & Mangun, G. R. (2009). *Cognitive Neuroscience: The biology of the mind.* New York, NY: W.W. Norton & Company.

Gere,C. (2013). Curating aphasia: Pierre Paul Broca's museological science. *Interdisciplinary Science Reviews*, 38(3). 200-2009. DOI: 10.1179/0308018813Z.00000000047

Gilligan, C. (1985/1993). *In a different voice: Psychological theory and women's development.* Cambridge, MA: Harvard University Press.

Gerrig, Richard J. & Philip G. Zimbardo. (2002.) Psychology And Life, 16/e . Published by Allyn and Bacon, Boston, MA: Pearson Education. Retrieved February 28, 2014, from http://www.apa.org/research/action/glossary.aspx

Goleman, D. (1995). *Emotional Intelligence.* New York, NY: Bantam Book.

———. (2006). *Social Intelligence: The New Science of Human Relationships.* New York, NY: Bantam Book.

Gopnik, A., & Wellman, H. M. (2012). Reconstructing constructivism: Causal models, Bayesian learning mechanism, and the theory theory. *Psychological Bulletin*, 138(6), 1085-1108. DOI: 10.1037/a0028044

Gopnik, A., Wellman, H. M., Gelman, S. A., & Neltzoff, A. N. (2010). A computational foundation for cognitive development: Comment on Griffths et al. and McLelland et al. *Trends in Cognitive Sciences*, 14(8), 342-364. DOI: 10.1016/j.tics.2010.05.012

Gusnard, D. A., Akbudak, E., Shulman, G., & Raichle, M. (2001). Medial prefrontal cortex and self-referencing mental activity: relation to a default mode of brain function. *Proceedings of the National Academy of Sciences of the United States of America*, 98(7), 4259-4264. DOI: 10.1073/pnas.071043098

Habib, R., Nyberg, L., & Tulving, E. (2003). Hemispheric asymmetries of memory: The HERA model revisited. *Trends in Cognitive Sciences,* 7(6), 241-245. DOI: 10.1016/S1364-6613(03)00110-4

Hagerty, J. (2014, May 10). How to train a herding puppy. *The Daily Puppy.* Retrieved from http://www.dailypuppy.com/articles/how-to-train-a-herding-puppy_802.html

Haier, R. (2009). What does a smart brain look like? *Scientific American Mind*, 20(6) 1-8. DOI: 10.1038/scientificamericanmind1109-26

Hamlin, J. K., & Wynn, K. (2011). Young infants prefer prosocial to antisocial others. *Cognitive Development,* 26(1), 30-39. DOI: 10.1016/j.cogdev.2010.09.001

Hamlin, J. K., Wynn, K., & Bloom, P. (2007). Social evaluation by preverbal infants. *Nature*, 450, 557-559. DOI: 10.1038/nature06288

Hazen, R. M. (2005). *Genesis: The scientific quest for life's origin.* Washington, DC, Joseph Henry Press.

Holland, J. H. (1998). *Emergence from chaos to order.* Cambridge, MA: Perseus Books.

Illinois State Board of Education. (2014, March 1). Illinois Learning Standards. Retrieved from http://www.isbe.net/ils/social_emotional/standards.htm

Jensen, E. (2006). *Enriching the brain: How to maximize every learner's potential.* San Francisco, CA: Jossey-Bass.

Jensen, E. (2008). *Brain-based learning: The new paradigm of teaching.* Thousand Oaks, CA: Corwin Books

John Upton Discovers the Need of Romaninan Orphans. (2009). Retrieved March 15, 2014, from ABC 20/20, http://www.youtube.com/watch?v=bvL_DGjGuhA

Jung, R. E., & Haier, R. (2007). The Parieto-Frontal IntegrationTtheory (P-FIT) of Intelligence: Converging neuroimaging evidence. *Behavioral and Brain Sciences*, 30(2) 135-187. DOI: 10.1017/S0140525X07001185.

Kadosh, R. C., Walsh, V., & Henik, A. (2007). Selecting between intelligent options. Commentary/Jung&Haier: Converging neuroimaging evidence. *Behavioral and Brain Sciences*, 30(2) 135-187. DOI: 10.1017/S0140525X07001203.

Khurana, V. G. (2006). *Brain surgery: A comprehensive and practical resource for brain surgery patients, their families and physicians.* Bloomington, IN: Author House.

Klingberg, T. (2010). Training and plasticity of working memory. *Trends in Cognitive Sciences*, 14(7), 317-324. DOI: 10.1016/j.tics.2010.05.002

Kohlberg, L. (1977). The implications of moral stage development for adult education. *Religious Education*, 72(2), 183-201. DOI: 10.1080/0034408770720209

Le Doux J. E. (2012). Rethinking the emotional brain. Neuron Perspective, 73(4), 653-675. DOI: 10.1016/j.neuron.2012.02.018

Le Doux, J. E. (2014). *Proceedings of the National Academy of Sciences of the United States of America.* 3(8), 2871-2878. DOI: 10.1073/pnas.1400335111.

Lee, Y., Lu, M. & Lo H. (2007). Effects of skill training on working memory capacity. *Learning and Instruction*, 17(3), 336-344. DOI: 10.1016/j.learninstruc.2007.02.010

Lehman, D.R., Lempert, R. O., & Nisbett, R. E. (1988). The effects of graduate training on reasoning: Formal discipline and thinking about everyday-life events. *American Psychologist*, 43(6), 431 442. DOI: 10.1037//0003-066x.43.6.431

Lieberman, M., (2013). *Social: Why our brains are wired to connect.* New York, NY: Crown.

Lightbrown, P. M., & Spada, N. (2006). *How languages are learned.* New York, NY: Oxford University Press.

Lucas, C. L., Bridgers, S., Grifflths, T. L., & Gopnik, A. (2014). When children are better (or at least more open-minded) learners than adults: Developmental differences in learning the forms of causal relationships. *Cognition*, 131 (2), 282-299. DOI: 10.1016/j.cognition.2013.12.010

Lyons, D. M., Price, E. O., & Moberg, G. P. (1988). Individual differences in temperament of domestic dairy goats: constancy and change. *Animal Behaviour*, 36 (5), 1323-1333. DOI: 10.1002/dev.420260503

Mayer, J. (2001). Interpersonal relations; Emotional intelligence. *Roeper Review*, 23 (3), 131. DOI: 10.1080/02783190109554084

May's Miracle. (2013). Retrieved March 27, 2014, from ABC 20/20, http://www.youtube.com/watch?v=RuO0B56evT0

Marieb, E.N., & Hoehn, K. (2013). *Human anatomy and physiology*. New York, NY: Pearson.

Mazzola, L., Isnard, J., Peyron, R., & Mauguiere, F. (2012). Stimulation of the human cortex and the experience of pain: Wilder Penfield observations revisited. Brain: *A Journal of Neurology*. 135(2), 631-640. DOI: 10.1093/brain/awr265.

McCarthy, C. (2008). *I'd rather teach peace*. New York, NY: Orbis Books.

McGonigal, K. (2012). *Maximum willpower: How to master the new science of self-control*. Oxford: Macmillan.

McGowan, P.O., Sasaki, A., Alessio A., Dymov, S., Labonte, B., Szyf, G. T., & Meaney, M. (2009). Epigenetic regulation of the glucocorticoid receptor in human brain associates with childhood abuse. *Nature Neruroscience*, 12(3), 342-348. DOI: 10.1038/nn.2270

McWhorter, J. H. (2012). *What language is and what it isn't and what it could be*. New York, NY: Gotham Books.

Meaney, M., Aitken, D. H., Bodmorr, S.R., Iny, L., & Tatarewicz, J.E. (2013a). Early Postnatal handling alters glucocorticoid receptor concentrations in selected brain regions. *Behavioral Neuroscience*, 127(5), 637-641. DOI: 1037/a0034187

Medline Plus. (2014, March 25). Retrieved from National Institute of Health: Http://www.nlm.nih.gov/medlineplus/

National Center for Biotechnology Information (1998). *Genes and Disease* [Internet]. Bethesda, MD: National Center for Biotechnology Information. Retrieved March 25, 2014, from http://www.ncbi.nlm.nih.gov/books/NBK22266/

Nicolas, S., Andrieu, B., Croizet, J.C., Sanitioso, R. B., & Burman, J. T. (2013). Sick? Or slow? On the origins of intelligence as a psychological object. *Intelligence*, 41(5), 699-711. DOI: 10.1016/j.intell.2013.08.006

Nishitani, N., & Hari, R. (2002). Viewing lipforms: Cortical dynamics. *Neuron*, 36(6), 1211-1220. DOI: 10.1016/S0896-6273(02)01089-9

Noddings, N. (1992). *The challenge to care in schools: An alternative approach to education*. New York, NY: Teachers College Press.

Ornaghi, V., Brockmeier, J., & Grazzani, I. (2014). Enhancing social cognition by training children in emotion understanding: A primary school study. *Journal of Experimental Child Psychology*, 119, 26-39. DOI: 10.1016/j.jecp.2013.10.005

Peake, P.K, Hebl, M., & Mischel, W. (2002). Strategic attention deployment for delar of gratification in working and waiting situations. *Developmental Psychology*, 38(2), 313-326. DOI: 10.1037//0012-1649.38.2.313

Piaget, J. (1971). *The origins of intelligence in children*. New York, NY: W.W. Norton & Company, Inc.

Pierce, B. A. (2005). *Genetics: A conceptual approach*. New York, NY: W. H. Freeman and Company.

Powers, K. E., Wagner, D. D., Norris, C. J., & Heatherton, T. F. (2011/2013). Socially excluded individuals fail to recruit medial prefrontal cortex for negative social scenes. *SCAN*, 8, 151-157. DOI: *10.1093/scan/nsr079*

Price, J. M., Colflesh, G. J. H., Cerella, J., & Verhaeghen, P. (2014). Making working memory work: The effects of extended practice on focus capcity and the processes of updating, forward access, and random access. *Acta Psychologica*, 148, 19-24. DOI: 10.1016/j.actpsy.2013.12.00810.1016/j.actpsy.2013.12.008

Rakoczy, H., Hamann, K., Warneken, F., & Tomasello, M. (2010). Bigger knows better: Young children selectively learn rule games from adults rather than from peers. *British Journal of Developmental Psychology*, 28(4), 785-798. DOI: 10.1348/026151009X479178

Richburg, M., & Fletcher, T. (2002). Emotional intelligence: Directing a child's emotional education. *Child Study Journal*, 32(1), 31-38.

Rizzolatti, G., & Craighero, L. (2004). The mirror-neuron system. *Annual Review Neuroscience*, 27, 169-192. DOI: 10.1146/annurev.neuro.27.070203.144230

Sapolsky, R. M. (1998). *Why zebras don't get ulcers: An updated guide to stress, stress-related diseases, and coping.* New York, NY: W. H. Freeman and Company.

Schnell, K., Bluschke, S., Konradt, B., & Walter, H. (2011). Functional relations of empathy and mentalizing: An fMRI study on the neural basis of cognitive empathy. *NeuroImage*, 54, 1743-1754. DOI: 10.1016/j.neuroimage.2010.08.024

Science Nation- Babies and Learning (2011). Retrieved March 10, 2014, from National Science Foundation, http://www.youtube.com/watch?v=F-UQkDs9I0I

Seaward, B. (2002). *Managing stress.* Boston, MA: Jones and Bartlett Publications.

Sharp, H., Pickles, A., Meaney, M., Marshall, K., Tibu, F., & Hill, J. (2012 a). Frequency of infant stroking reported by mothers moderates the effect of prenatal depression on infant behavioral and physiological outcomes. *PLOS ONE*, 7(10) e45446. DOI: 10.1371/journal.pone.0045446

Sherman, P. W. & Alcock, J. (2010). *Animal behavior: Exploring animal behavior: Readings from the American scientist.* Sunderland, MA: Sinauer Associates.

Shiv, B., & Nowlis, S. M. (2004). The effect of distractions while tasting a food sample: The interplay of informational and affective components in subsequent choice. *Journal of Consumer Research*, 31(3), 599-608. DOI: 10.1086/425095

Shoda, Y., Mischel, W., & Peake, P.K. (1990). Predicting adolescent cognitive and self-regulatory competencies from preschool delay of gratification: Identifying diagnostic conditions. *Developmental Psychology*, 26(6), 978-986. DOI: 10.1037//0012-1649.26.6.978

Singer, T., & Frith, C. (2005). The painful side of empathy. *News and Views*, 8(7), 845-846. DOI:10.1038/nn0705-845

Singer, T., Seymour, B., O'Doherty, J., Stephan, K., Dolan, R. & Frith, C. (2006). Empathic neural responses are modulated by the perceived fairness of others. *Nature*, 439(26), 466-469. DOI:10.1038/nature04271

Sprenger, M. (1999). *Learning and memory: The brain in action*. Alexandria, VA: ASCD.

Standing, L. G. (1973). Learning 10,000 pictures. *Quarterly journal of Experimental Psychology*, 25, 207-222. DOI: 10.1080/14640747308400340

Standing, L. G., & Bertrand (2008). Effects of size congruency on item and size recognition with words or pictures. *Perceptual and Motor Skills*, 107(6), 449-456. DOI: 10.2466/pms.107.6.449-456

Stolt, S., Korja, R., Matomaki, J., Lapinleimu, H., Haataja, L., & Lehtonen, L. (2014). Early relations between language development and the quality of mother-child interaction in very-low-birth-weight children. *Early Human Development*, 90, 219-225. DOI: 10.1016/j.earlhumdev.2014.02.007

Suderman, M., McGowan, P.O., Sasaki, A., Huang, T., Hallett, M, Meaney, M., Turecki, G., & Szyf, M. (2012b). Conserved epigenetic sensitivity to early life experience in the rat and human hippocampus. *PNAS*, 109, 17266-17272. DOI: 10.1073/pnas.1121260109

Swimme, B. (1984). *The universe is a green dragon: A cosmic creation story.* Santa Fe, NM: Bear and Company.

Thurman, R. A. F. (2005). *Anger.* New York, NY: Oxford University Press.

Tomasello, M. (2000). Culture and cognitive development. *American Psychological Society*, 9(2), 37-40. DOI: 10.1111/1467-8721.00056

Tomasello, M., Carpenter, M., Call, J., Behne, T., & Moll, H. (2005) Understanding and sharing intentions: The origins of cultural cognition. *The Behavioral and Brain Sciences*, 28(5), 691-735. DOI: 10.1017/S0140525X05000129

Tomson, A., Cook, C. H., Guerrini, I., Sheedy, D., Harper, C., Marshall, E. J. (2008). Wernicke's Encephalopathy Revisited. Translation of the case history section of the original manuscript by Carl Wernicke "Lehrbuch der Gehirn-rankheiten fur Aerzte and Studirende" (1881) with a commentary. Alcohol and Alcoholism, 43(2), 174-179. *PMID*: 18056751. DOI: 10.1093/alcalc/agm149

Traviss, M. P. (1985). *Student moral development in the catholic school.* Washington, DC: The National Catholic Educational Association.

Tulving, E. (2002). Episodic memory: From mind to brain. *Annual Review Psychology*, 53, 1-25. DOI: 10.1146/annurev.psych.53.100901.135114

Tulving E., & Markowitsch, H. J. (1998). Episodic and declarative memory: Role of the hippocampus. *Hippocampus*, 8(3), 198-204. DOI: 10.1002/(SICI)1098-1063(1998)8:3 198::AID-HIPO2 3.0.CO;2-G

Viadero, D. (1998). Research notes. *Education Week*, 18(11), 28-29.

Vygotsky, L. S. (1978). *Mind in society: The development of higher psychologicalprocesses*. Cambridge, MA: Harvard University Press.

Wagner, R. K., & Sternberg, R. J. (1985). Practical intelligence in real-world pursuits: The role of tacit knowledge. *Journal of Personality and Social Psychology*, 48(2), 436-458.

Willis J. (2006). *Research-based strategies to ignite student learning.* Alexandria, VA: ASCD

Wilmore, J. H., Costill, D. L., & Kenney, W. L. (2008). *Physiology of sport and exercise.* Champaign, IL: Human Kinetics.

Westerberg, H., & Klingberg, T. (2007). Changes in cortical activity after training of working memory-a single subject analysis. *Physiology & Behavior*, 92, 186-192. DOI: 10.1016/j.physbeh.2007.05.041

Woolfolk, A. (2013). *Educational psychology.* New York, NY: Pearson.

Zhang, T.Y., Labonte, B., Wen Z. L., Turecki, g., & Meaney M. (2013b). Epigenetic mechanisms for the early environmental regulation of hippocampal glucocorticoid receptor gene expression in rodents and humans. *Neuropsychopharmacology Reviews*, 38, 111-123. *Neuropsychopharmacology Reviews* (2013) 38, 111–123; doi:10.1038/npp.2012.149; published online 12 September 2012

Zwickel, J., White, S. J., Coniston, D., Senju, A., & Frith, U. (2011). Exploring the building block of social cognition: Spontaneous agency perception and visual perspective taking in autism. *SCAN*, 6, 564-571.

Soc Cogn Affect Neurosci (2011) 6 (5): 564-571. doi: 10.1093/scan/nsq088

Index